100 Great Paintings

in The Victoria & Albert Museum

PUBLICATION MADE POSSIBLE BY UNITED TECHNOLOGIES CORPORATION

Published by the Victoria and Albert Museum, 1985
© The Trustees of the Victoria and Albert Museum
Designed by Derek Birdsall R.D.I.
Typesetting by Balding + Mansell Limited in Monophoto Van Dijck
Colour origination by Peak Litho Plates
Printed in England by Penshurst Press using Inmont Inks

ISBN 0-905209-49-4 (Faber)

Contents

CONTRIBUTORS

C.M.K.	Michael Kauffmann
J.M.	John Murdoch
H.B.	Harold Barkley
M.H-B.	Mark Haworth-Booth
L.L.	Lionel Lambourne
J.D.H.	Jean Hamilton
R.M.	Rosemary Miles
C.N.	Charles Newton
M.S.	Michael Snodin
M.W.T.	Margaret Timmers
A.B.	Anne Buddle
S.C.	Stephen Calloway
C.P.T.	Christopher Titterington
E.C.	Elizabeth Clunas
K.H.J.C.	Howard Coutts
A.N.	Alex Noble
S.P.	Sarah Postgate
G.M.S.	Gillian Saunders
B.B.	Barbara Bodgener
M.G.	Marilyn Gasparini
M.R.K.	Martin Kauffmann

This book was conceived as a means of introducing the V&A's fine collection of paintings to a wider audience. The role of the V&A as a collector of paintings has perhaps been obscured by its reputation as a museum of the decorative arts. With the Department of Prints, Drawings, Paintings and Photographs now established in splendid new premises in the Henry Cole wing – and many of the pictures included here on permanent display for the first time – this book is a valuable and timely introduction to the unexpected range and richness of the collection.

We have been fortunate in finding in United Technologies Corporation an enthusiastic and committed sponsor. Without them this elegant publication would not have been possible.

I am grateful to those who have worked so hard on the production of this book, particularly to Nicky Bird whose idea it was, Derek Birdsall for his excellent design, Will Allan who co-ordinated the project, Sally Chappell for the photography and Gill Saunders who nursed the project through its long gestation period, organising photography and orchestrating the other contributors. And we are indebted, as ever, to Julie Laird of the V&A Associates for arranging sponsorship of this splendid volume, as she does for so many of the Museum's books, exhibitions and galleries.

SIR ROY STRONG
Director
Victoria & Albert Museum
London

We are happy to help make possible the publication of this handsome presentation of the paintings in one of the world's great museums. It is a work long overdue, and one we hope will be long enjoyed

HARRY J. GRAY
Chairman
United Technologies Corporation

9

Introduction

Because the name of the V&A is most closely associated with the decorative arts, it may come as a surprise to many visitors to learn that the Museum's Paintings Department holds some 2,000 oil and tempera paintings, 6,000 water-colours and 2,000 miniatures. And yet the truism remains: this is not the National Gallery or the Tate, its history is very different and these differences are reflected in the selection of paintings reproduced in this book.

The collection owes its origin to the munificent gift of John Sheepshanks (1787–1863). A Leeds clothing manufacturer long settled in London, he had become a friend of a wide circle of contemporary artists and entertained the vision of establishing a national gallery of British art to parallel the National Gallery, founded in 1824. Accordingly, in 1857 he presented to the South Kensington Museum 233 oil paintings and 298 water-colours and drawings. Although he had bought some fine works from Constable and Turner, his personal favourites were the genre painters who had risen to fame in this country in the early 19th century in parallel with the growing popularity of Dutch 17th-century figure subjects: Wilkie, Mulready, Landseer, C R Leslie, William Collins, Richard Redgrave – these were the artists most patronised by Sheepshanks and they give the Museum's collection its distinctive character. Richard Redgrave, author of a *Century of British Painters* and a Royal Academian, became the collection's first Keeper and its expansion after Sheepshanks' gift owes much to his energy and discrimination.

By gift and bequest, more than by purchase, the collection was subsequently extended until the galleries provided the visitor

with an unbroken representation of the British School from the early 18th to the later 19th century. However, it was only in 1888 with the gift of Isobel Constable, the painter's youngest surviving daughter, of 95 oil sketches and 297 drawings and water-colours by John Constable that the collection acquired its present distinctive character and status. Acquisitions became fewer after the turn of the century and in 1908 the function of national Gallery of British Art was transferred to the newly founded Tate Gallery.

Meanwhile, European paintings had also been acquired, though on a smaller scale and for a different purpose. From the earliest years of the Museum's history, J C Robinson, the indefatigable Art Referee, was scouring the Continent for works of art recently torn from their original homes in churches and palaces, and many of these purchases were of paintings. These were bought to fulfil the Museum's function as a storehouse of decoration and design, "to show the application of fine art to objects of utility", and they included gothic altarpieces and Italian crucifixes, banners and cassone panels, quite different to the easel pictures acquired at the same time by the National Gallery. These works still form an important part of the Museum's Primary Galleries where they amplify the collections of sculpture and the decorative arts. Within this context also, the Museum provided an obvious home for the great cartoons by Raphael for the tapestries in the Sistine Chapel, which were placed there on permanent loan from the royal collection in 1864.

For later periods, the strengths of the collection reflect the personal taste of individual donors: John Jones (1882) for the

French 18th century, represented here by De Troy, Boucher and Lancret; The Rev C H Townshend, (1868) a friend of Dickens who wintered in Lausanne and patronized contemporary Swiss and German painters; and, above all, Constantine Alexander Ionides (1900) whose masterpieces by Le Nain, Delacroix, Degas, Burne-Jones and Rossetti are reproduced in this book.

The acquisition of oil paintings other than of those linked with decorative schemes – such as Hayman's for Vauxhall Gardens – effectively came to an end at the turn of the century. However, for both British water-colours and portrait miniatures the Museum has continued to hold the national collections and acquisitions by both gift and purchase have continued on a considerable scale. The portrait miniatures, which were used for personal adornment in the form of lockets or in conjunction with jewellery, are linked with the V&A's jewellery and costume collections as much as with the history of British painting. Here, the outstanding bequest was that of George Salting in 1910 which contains Holbein's *Anne of Cleves* and ten miniatures by Nicholas Hilliard, including the famous *Young man leaning against a tree among roses*, one of the most beguiling and sophisticated works in the whole of Elizabethan art. Portrait miniatures, indeed, have provided a consistently strong element in British painting, as the work of Hilliard, Isaac Oliver, Samuel Cooper and the 18th-century practitioners, such as Engleheart, Smart and Cosway, serves to testify.

The collection of British water-colours is comprehensive in the sense not only of holding examples by every significant artist in the field but also of including masterpieces by the outstanding ones – Sandby, Cozens, Girtin, Turner, Cotman, Blake, Palmer and Cox – to mark the turning points and milestones against which the more routine products can be placed. Under Richard Redgrave's discriminating eye, major collections of both 18th- and 19th-century water-colours were acquired by gift and bequest, including those of William Smith, F.S.A. (1871) and the Rev Alexander Dyce (1869), and purchase. Most 19th-century acquisitions were of the "golden period" of English water-colour, 1780–1840, but subsequently water-colours of the Pre-Raphaelites and the later 19th-century painters also entered the collection.

The 20th-century holdings again owe a great deal to private benefactors: for example to Capt Lionel Guy Baker for the group of Vorticist works by Wyndham Lewis and to Margaret Nash and the Nash Trust for a representative collection of water-colours by Paul Nash. Since about 1960, more consistent efforts have been made to bring the 20th-century collection up to date and to buy major works by Continental and American artists – Nolde, Klee and Sam Francis are reproduced here – against which the achievements of the British School may be judged. The artists representing the last twenty-five years of work in this country – Eduardo Paolozzi, Peter Blake, Richard Smith and Tom Phillips – have been chosen at random to convey something of the strength and rapid growth of the collection in this most stimulating of all fields.

Dr.Michael Kauffmann
Keeper of Paintings
Victoria and Albert Museum
1984

Umbrian School late 12th century
PAINTED CRUCIFIX, WITH MARY AND ST. JOHN
Tempera on canvas on panel, 218.5 × 171.5 cm
850–1900. *Gift of Lord Carmichael.*

Italian paintings produced before 1300 are exceptionally rare; it has been estimated that over ninety per cent of very early Italian paintings have not survived into the present century. This crucifix is the most important Italian painting of its period in a British collection, and gives us a glimpse of what painting in Italy was like before Cimabue, Giotto and Duccio made the innovations and refinements in Tuscan painting in the early 14th century that are generally considered to mark the beginning of modern Western painting.

The Church was the dominant cultural influence of this time, and virtually all the surviving Italian pictures of this date are religious in character. Painted crucifixes such as these were intended as devotional pieces to be hung above the screen or an altar, or to be carried in procession, and act as aids to religious contemplation to anyone praying in the church or attending mass. This crucifix impresses us by the stark simplicity with which its main features are drawn. Christ hangs before us; He confronts us with open eyes and He exposes the wounds on His hands and feet to our view. On His left is St. John the Evangelist and on His right the Virgin who indicates him to the spectator with her hands. At His hands and feet are three scenes; on the left, the Harrowing of Hell, on the right Holy Women at the Sepulchre, and at the bottom the Denial of St. Peter. These scenes are intended to remind the spectator of the human frailty of doubting Christ's sacrifice

and His ultimate power to rise above death and ultimately to help the spectator gain eternal life by having faith in Christ's sacrifice and resurrection. The point is underlined by the top terminal of the crucifix, where Christ is shown victorious with two angels.

All the features of the crucifix are painted with the utmost simplicity, as is usual in paintings of this date; the draperies fall in simple folds and the heads are drawn like simple masks with no attempt to give them any expression. Later depictions of this scene (post 1250) were to show a specific moment of the crucifixion, with Christ dead, His eyes closed and His body slumped down the cross, and the Virgin and St. John conspicuously grieving at the sides of the cross. This early cross eschews any such dramatic representation of the event and portrays a collection of artistically somewhat disconnected scenes and figures which serve as "clues" to the spectator to reconstruct his own personal conception of the agony of the crucifixion and the immensity of Christ's sacrifice.

This panel is fairly well-preserved, considering its age, though there are losses of paint on the Virgin's robe and the little scenes at the terminals of the cross. Few individual painters of this period are known by name, but it displays a mixture of central Italian motifs that suggest that it was painted in Umbria in the last quarter of the twelfth century. K.H.J.C.

Barnaba da Modena active 1361–83
Italian School
PROCESSIONAL BANNER: THE CRUCIFIXION WITH THE VIRGIN,
ST. JOHN AND ST. ANTHONY ABBOTT ON THE FRONT AND
SAINTS ANTHONY ABBOTT AND ELIGIUS ADORED BY MEMBERS
OF A CONFRATERNITY ON THE BACK
Tempera on canvas, 197 × 128 cm
781–1894

The identity of this painting as a processional banner may
be readily inferred from its salient characteristics. It is on
canvas – a medium used for hardly any other purpose in the
14th century – it is painted on both sides, it depicts members
of the group that carried it, and its size accords well with
its function. The border containing saints and prophets in
medallions was probably typical of such banners, which could
obviously not have an ordinary wooden frame. However,
comparisons are difficult, for hardly any other 14th-century
banners survive.

Although both sides are attributed to Barnaba da Modena,
who was the leading painter in Genoa in the 1360s and 70s,
they do appear very different in style. The saints' unusually
awesome, dark faces, with strong white highlights, and the
gold striation on otherwise flat drapery point to a very
close dependence on the Italo-Byzantine tradition of the
13th century. The contrast with the Crucifixion is striking.
The faces are lighter, their expressions less sternly hieratic,
and the draperies are modelled to give the appearance of
considerable bulk. In short, the Crucifixion shows the influence
of the Tuscan tradition of the 14th century, which is so
notably lacking in the portrayal of the two saints. Such a
stylistic dichotomy is rare in a single work, but both styles
occur in Barnaba's paintings. His tenacious adherence to the
Italo-Byzantine style gave way in the 1370s to a more modern
style influenced by Tuscan painting and hence a date c.1370
may be proposed for this banner.

St. Anthony Abbot carries his main attributes, a Tau cross and a bell. St. Eligius, patron of goldsmiths and blacksmiths, is holding a butteris used for paring horses' hoofs, and a severed horse's leg – a reference to the story of how he drove the devil from a vicious horse by cutting off its leg, making the sign of the Cross and sticking it on again. The kneeling worshippers wear a white, hooded habit with a circle cut out at the back. This is the habit of the lay confraternities of Flagellants; the holes at the back existed to facilitate the task of self chastisement. As St. Anthony Abbot appears on both the front and the back he was presumably the principal patron of this confraternity, and there was indeed a confraternity of Flagellants in Genoa dedicated to him, for whom this banner was most probably made. One of this confraternity's appointed tasks was healing the sick and burying the dead. This explains the presence of St. Eligius, a 7th-century French bishop whose good works included burial of the dead. Both the penitential character of the Flagellant confraternities and their dedication to the sick and dying should be seen in the context of the Black Death of 1348 and the continued epidemics that swept western Europe in the late 14th century.   C.M.K.

Nardo di Cione active 1343; d.1365/66
Florentine School
THE CORONATION OF THE VIRGIN
Tempera on panel, 118 × 77.5 cm
CAI. 104. *Ionides Bequest.*

It is perhaps a truism to say that museums inevitably display their objects somewhat divorced from their original context and function. This panel of 'The Coronation of the Virgin', for example, would in all probability once have formed the central panel of a large polyptych (that is, an altarpiece of many panels separated by the framing) that would have graced some Florentine chapel. It would probably have been surrounded by side panels of saints, and at the bottom there might have been a 'predella' or series of small narrative panels depicting scenes from the lives of the saints or Christ. Furthermore we cannot be sure that it is the whole of the central panel that we see before us today, since similar representations of the scene usually show a group of angels seated on the steps below the Virgin and Christ.

The subject of The Coronation of the Virgin achieved great popularity in 14th-century Italy, in line with the growth of the cult of the Virgin Mary. The basic pattern in Florence for the subject was Giotto's *Baroncelli Polyptych* of the second quarter of the 14th century. Nardo has followed Giotto in the pose of the two main figures fairly closely, but has completely altered the effect of the picture by his careful attention to the details of the scene, such as the Virgin's modest downward-looking gaze, and the adoption as a floor-covering of the beautiful blue, red and gold cloth on the step below. This design is derived from near-Eastern textiles and is indicative of the increasing interest of the generation of painters after Giotto in purely decorative aspects of painting. This tendency was eventually to lead to the full-blown late Gothic style of Gentile da Fabriano and Pisanello of the early 15th-century.

The panel is in good condition, a tribute to the surety of the craftsmanship of Florentine painters of the 14th century. A description of their techniques can be found in the near-contemporary *Libro d'Arte* of Cennino Cennini. First the carpentry and gilding of the whole altarpiece was undertaken, a thin layer of gesso (fine plaster) being laid over the wooden panels to ensure a smooth surface. Then the figures themselves would have been painted in, in the medium of tempera, where egg-white is used to bind the pigment. Finally the blue of Christ's robe would have been laid in, the pigment being made of powdered lapis-lazuli. The whole process was extremely expensive and involved many different hands; to this extent such paintings were as much the product of a workshop as an individual hand. It was only with the coming of oil paints and canvas supports to Italy in the later 15th century that artists were able to develop more personal conceptions of a theme and depart from the patterns and techniques laid down by their masters generations before.

Nardo di Cione was, with his brothers Andrea (called Orcagna) and Jacopo a member of one of the largest workshops in Florence in the middle of the 14th century. They aimed to consolidate the gains in representational painting made by Giotto earlier in the century, but added to it an interest in new themes, such as the frescoes in the Strozzi Chapel of Santa Maria Novella of the Last Judgement, Paradise and Hell, and a concern for fine craftsmanship and technique. *The Coronation of the Virgin* well sums up the lucidity and the quality of the work that they produced.   K.H.J.C.

18

Marzal de Sas active 1393–after 1410
Spanish (Valencian) School
PANEL FROM AN ALTARPIECE OF ST. GEORGE:
ST. GEORGE TIES UP THE DRAGON
Tempera and gilt on pine panel
1217–1864

This is one of seventeen panels forming part of a large altar-piece showing scenes from the life of St. George. It was painted probably by Marzal de Sas, the leading painter in Valencia, in about 1410–20, for the Centenar de la Ploma, a confraternity of Civic Militia consisting of 100 archers of which George was the patron saint. For its sheer size (6.6 × 5.5 m), visual impact and excellent state of preservation, it is one of the most famous objects in the Museum.

According to the *Life of St. George* as recounted in the *Golden Legend*, the town of Silene, Libya, was threatened by a dragon, which could only be pacified by the daily sacrifice of a human being and a sheep. When the lot fell upon the king's daughter, the king was forced to give her up, in spite of his protests. It so happened that St. George was riding by just as the dragon was approaching its victims, whereupon he promptly pierced it with his lance. Next follows the scene reproduced here. St. George, now dismounted, is tying up the dragon with the princess's girdle, while the king and queen and the inhabitants of Silene watch from the city walls. The defeated dragon, now quite tamed, is then led back to the city, and the inhabitants of Silene are so impressed that the king, queen and princess and 15,000 men are baptised. The following pictures concern St. George's persecution by Dacian, the local ruler, including six scenes of the most fearful tortures, before he is finally beheaded.

This, then, is the most charming scene on the altarpiece and it stands in strong contrast to the gruesome tortures depicted below it. It epitomizes the essential characteristics of the International Gothic style of about 1400: grace and elegance, together with a growing concern for a more accurate depiction of nature. The princess, young and pretty, is very fashionably dressed in a high waisted *hopa*, or cassock, of brocade edged with ermine, with long sleeves reaching nearly to the ground. The sumptuous brocade consists of floral designs on a gold ground intricately punched with dots; the remainder of the surface is painted red, leaving the floral pattern reserved in gold. The technique of punching the gold with a myriad of dots to achieve the rich effect of brocade is typical of Valencian painting of this period. St. George wears a white silk shirt with a red cross on the front and back which was in fact the uniform of the members of the Centenar de la Ploma who had commissioned the altarpiece. Interest in a natural setting is expressed in the plant studies, and in the theatre-set perspective of the city, which marks the extent and the limit of realism in Western painting at the period immediately preceding the 'new realism' of Jan van Eyck.   C.M.K.

PANEL A
Florentine School c.1430
CASSONE PANEL WITH SCENES OF A MARRIAGE CEREMONY,
WITH (CENTRE) AN ALLEGORICAL FIGURE OF CONSTANCY
HOLDING A COLUMN AND A SCROLL INSCRIBED NON MUOVA
(?) IL COR MEO (MY HEART REMAINS CONSTANT)
Gilt gesso and tempera on panel 45.7 × 134.6 cm
5791–1860

These panels were once part of chests (*cassone*), meaningfully painted with representations of heroic or moralising themes or marriage ceremonies, and commissioned in pairs to celebrate a marriage.

The two left-hand scenes on Panel A may depict Boccaccio's story of Patient Griselda, who endured many trials after her marriage, and was eventually accorded her lord's respect and devotion. However, neither Boccaccio nor any other known representations of his story include the third scene. The source might be an unidentified literary theme, but since the same figures appear in all three scenes, it is probable that these represent a marriage ceremony.

PANEL B

WORKSHOP OF APOLLONIO DI GIOVANNI

Florentine School

CASSONE PANEL: THE CONTINENCE OF SCIPIO

Tempera on poplar, 43.5 × 133 cm

5804–1859

The Continence of Scipio (Panel B), was a subject rarely depicted by 15th-century artists, even on cassone. Classical authors relate how Scipio, whose name, 'Scipione', is inscribed on his hat, desired Lucretia as his own. However when informed of her betrothal to Allucius, Scipio nobly restored Lucretia to him, and returned to her parents her ransom of gold. Thus, beside the oriental carpet, stands a gold chest. True nobility lies, not in wealth and status – 'Seven or eight yards of scarlet will make a new citizen,' remarked Cosimo de Medici – but in the Renaissance ideal of exemplary virtue.

The confident treatment of architecture and perspective in Figure B (c.1463–70) is that of Florence's leading workshop

and its master, Apollonio de Giovanni. Its uninterrupted, rectangular format reflects Alberti's recommendations in *Della Pittura*, also a desirable affinity with classical sarcaphogi, and familiarity with Ghiberti's doors for the Florentine Baptistry. Ghiberti had abandoned cusped quatrefoils for unified compositions, one of which, Solomon and the Queen of Sheba, is reflected on two other cassone in the Museum. The earlier Florentine panel (c.1430), possibly from the workshop of the Master of the Grigg's Crucifixion, has a two-dimensional quality. It retains the cusped divisions characteristic of the Gothic style, and medieval symbolism is perpetuated in the figure of Constancy, with column and inscribed scroll.

Muted reds and greens predominate in Panel A; gilding is restricted to the surrounding carved gesso panels. The Scipio panel glistens with gold, applied by the *mettodoro* after the painter had worked the colours. These are more varied, reflecting light and shade, and further embellished with punched motifs, a technique also used on small Renaissance caskets in the Museum, and by all *cassone* workshops.   A.B.

Workshop of Apollonio di Giovanni
Florentine School
BIRTH TRAY: THE TRIUMPH OF LOVE
REVERSE: SHIELD WITH TWO ARMS FRAMED BY A GARLAND
Tempera on poplar panel, 12-sided. Diam 59.7 cm; diam.,
including frame 73 cm; thickness of panel 3.2 cm
144–1869

Renaissance workshops produced not only *cassoni* (see above), but also painted banners, wainscot panels, bed-heads and birth-trays (*deschi da parto*). *Deschi* were commissioned to celebrate a birth, when ceremonial gifts were presented to the mother, and were subsequently preserved as commemorative objects – at Lorenzo de Medici's death (1493), his *desco* was found in the chamber.

This example was painted in Apollonio di Giovanni's workshop. A 17th-century copy of Apollonio's *bottega* (account book) affords a fascinating insight into contemporary social history: a record 23 pairs of cassoni produced in 1452, and, beside the clients' names, orders for *deschi* closely follow those for *cassoni*. To achieve and maintain this output, techniques and designs were standardized. Stock figures include the elegant youth in ¾-frontal pose, and the same regal female representing Juno, the Queen of Sheba or Lucretia. The delightful seascape, like the city on Panel B above, is a compilation of workshop models, and hats and head-dresses conform to standard types.

Cupid on his triumphal car is a scene inspired by Petrarch's *Trionfi*. Before c.1450, illustrations to The Triumph of Love had included the chariot, based on classical models, but not,

as here, the humorous scenes of Phyllis riding Aristotle, and Delilah shearing Samson. These scenes of female domination had themselves been represented earlier – they were popular in France, and occur in a 14th-century German embroidery – but their association with The Triumph of Love possibly originated in two manuscript illustrations by Apollonio. Extolled by a contemporary poet as 'The Tuscan Apelles', Apollonio's significance in disseminating representations of subjects inspired by classical antiquity was considerable.

A preoccupation with heraldry in Early Renaissance architecture and decoration reflects the significance attached to marriage and childbirth in competitive society. Within a garland comparable to those on the Museum's terra-cotta heraldic plaques by Luca della Robbia, the *desco* bears on the reverse the arms of the Samminiato and Gianfigliazzi families. No liaison between these families is recorded before 1537, and yet the Triumph scene, on stylistic grounds, must date from c.1460. Although the *desco* may have been associated with an earlier, unrecorded marriage, the back was probably repainted after the 1537 marriage. However, this destroyed the original coat of arms, and the first owner's identity is now lost.

A.B.

Sandro Botticelli 1444/5–1510
Italian (Florentine) School
SMERALDA BANDINELLI, GRANDMOTHER OF THE SCULPTOR
BACCIO BANDINELLI, C.1471
Tempera on panel, 65.7 × 41 cm
CAI.100. *Ionides Bequest.*

This is a typical early Botticelli portrait and the identity of the sitter is firmly established by the inscription on the window frame.

The sitter wears a summer at-home costume comprising a white silk or linen *camisa*, generously cut as the many folds at the neck and sleeves show; a *cotta* of red silk, slit and laced fashionably at the forearms to reveal the *camisa*; and, overall, a *gonella* or summer overgown, of sheer gold-edged fabric with loose cuffs and open from the waist to show the silk beneath.

Sumptuary laws, first introduced in Italy in the early 14th century, attempted to limit extravagant dress. Smeralda would have been allowed only two overgowns of silk in her wardrobe and only one overgown dyed with the rare red kermes dye we see here. The approved garments would have been marked and would have been worn for at least three years.

Over her shoulders and tucked into the neckline is a sheer silk kerchief. As befitting a young married woman, another covers her neatly confined hair. This kerchief should also be sheer but seems to have been overpainted in the 19th century. A delicate metalwork necklace of the type popular in the late 15th century circles her neck. She holds the white, embroidered handkerchief of a refined lady. Less wealthy women wore similar clothes, only cut less fully and of coarser materials.

The window shutter projecting strangely through an opening behind her may, with the column, shallow setting, and uneven number of lacings at her wrists, add up to a personal symbolism of the kind seen in other Botticelli portraits.

Her quiet dignity recalls the contemporary description by Lorenzo the Magnificent of his Ideal Beauty: 'Her beauty, as I have said was wonderful . . . the tone of her complexion was white yet not pallid, fresh yet not glowing. Her face was grave yet not proud, sweet and pleasing, not frivolous or light-hearted. Her eyes were animated and motionless with no trace of conceit or meanness . . . She dressed in those fashions which suited a noble and gentle lady . . .' (J. Herald, *Renaissance Dress in Italy, 1400–1500*, London, 1981, p.157–8)

This sort of beauty appealed to another poet 400 years later: The Pre-Raphaelite poet and admirer of Botticelli, Dante Gabrielle Rossetti. Rossetti purchased the portrait in 1867 when Botticelli had just been 'rediscovered'. He sold the painting in the early 1880's, probably to Constantine Ionides, who bequeathed it to the Museum. M.G.

Carlo Crivelli active 1457–94
Venetian School
VIRGIN AND CHILD
Signed on edge of parapet: OPUS. CA ROLI. CRIVELLI. VENETI
Tempera on panel, 48.5 × 33.6 cm
492–1882. *John Jones Bequest.*

Conspicuous in the composition, the inscription proclaims as the artist the Venetian, Carlo Crivelli. The image is typical of Venetian 'madonniera' – sophisticated, reflective figures – and this, together with its small size, suggests that the painting was never part of an altarpiece, but intended for private devotion.

Crivelli left Venice in 1458, and from 1468 lived and travelled in the Marches, distanced from mainstream artistic currents, and from his contemporaries, Bellini and the Vivarinis. In this provincial environment, Crivelli achieved a considerable reputation, and was knighted in 1490 by Ferdinand II.

The decorative qualities of the picture – the exaggerated elegance of tapering fingers; elongated eyelids; the mantle's sweeping, protective curve, echoed by the Virgin's head – evoke the International Gothic style. Crivelli would have known Gentile da Fabriano's paintings in the Doge's Palace at Venice, and here depicts equally sumptuous fabrics, but also captures the fragile transparency of the Virgin's veil and undergarment, peeping out from beneath her sleeve.

Unlike many of his contemporaries, Crivelli never abandoned tempera colours to experiment with oil-based medium. Flat pattern and pure vivid colours – the green lining

juxtaposed with the mantle's varnished gold; brilliant red under the swaddling bands – are combined with a hard linear clarity, detailed realism, architectural features and festoons of fruit. Here, Mantegna's influence is apparent, and Crivelli's leafless tree echoes those of Mantegna and Bellini. The garland, ultimately of classical origin, is derived from Donatello, who visited Padua in 1444. The use of large areas of gold, with elaborate patterns in relief, is a characteristic archaism, perpetuating, but reinterpreting the Byzantine style.

Italian Renaissance artists had eschewed symbolism in their search for greater scientific realism, and the carnation, violets and fly show Flemish influence. The composition itself, a half-length portrait figure with parapet or sill, was introduced by van Eyck, c.1430, and Eyckian also is Crivelli's minute observation of detail. The fly, disseminator of disease, is equated with Sin: 'Beware,' said Bernard of Siena, 'that the fly of Sin never enters in.' Of the violet, he says, 'Mary is the violet of Humility'. Pomegranates and phoenix symbolize Resurrection and Life; the Child's apple, Christ's Incarnation, and the carnation His Passion. The cracked sill symbolizes the veil of the Temple, rent in two at Christ's death, and the vine, symbolizing the redeeming blood of Christ, climbs up the dead tree, around which fly two birds, symbolizing the souls of men.

A.B.

30

Master of the St. Ursula Legend active c.1480–c.1510
School of Cologne
THE MARTYRDOM OF ST. URSULA AND THE 11,000 VIRGINS,
c.1492–6
Oil on canvas, 165 × 186.7 cm
5938–1867

St. Ursula and her 11,000 companions returned to Cologne
from their pilgrimage to Rome just at the time when,
unbeknown to them, the Huns were besieging the city.
As soon as they disembarked, the Huns leapt upon them with
savage cries and the massacre began. St. Ursula is shown
holding her bridegroom who is pierced with a sword.
The leader of the Huns on the right is willing to stop the
massacre if Ursula would consent to marry him, but she refuses
and is martyred together with her companions, while the
angels carry their souls to heaven.

Careful attention has been paid to topographical accuracy in
representing the city of Cologne: each of the buildings can be
readily identified. The large church of St. Martin dominates on
the banks of the Rhine; the tower of the city hall adjoins the
great cathedral and the church of St. Gereon appears on the
right of the tent. Below, two pairs of donors are identified by
inscription as Wynant van Wickroid, his wife Lysbet,
and Heinrich van Wickroid with his wife Hilgen.

This is the largest of nineteen pictures of the life of St. Ursula,
which are scattered in various museums, mainly in Germany,
by an artist whose name we do not know, but who is called
'Master of the St. Ursula Legend' from this series. He is one of

the principal painters of the Cologne School at the end of its
period of greatness. His ability to endow his figures with
convincingly individual features and expression and to render
architecture in a wholly realistic manner links his work with
Netherlandish painting, which was very influential in Cologne
throughout the 15th century. Perhaps his most individual
contribution lies in conveying distance, atmosphere and light,
to an extent unusual before 1500.

This St. Ursula series is of particular interest, as it has been
possible to identify the donors, who were shown at the foot of
each of them, with actual citizens of Cologne recorded in the
city archives. It was they who paid for these pictures to be
hung in a church, probably St. Bridget's. The donors of the
Martyrdom, Wynant and Heinrich van Wickroid,
were brothers: Wynant was a tax collector, Heinrich a silk
weaver, city councillor and magistrate in the 1480s and 90s.
His wife, Hilgen, was also an independent silk weaver;
she married in 1492/3 and died some four years later.
They belonged to the class of wealthy manufacturers and
tradesmen that provided much of the artistic patronage, not
only in Cologne, but also in the other commercial centres of
15th-century Germany.   C.M.K.

Gönant vä vickroid. lysbet hin huysfrau ⸱—⸱

Hajnrich vä vickroid. hilge hin huisfrau

Raphael 1483–1520
Italian (Roman) School
THE MIRACULOUS DRAUGHT OF FISHES
Body colour on paper laid on to canvas, 319 × 399 cm
On loan from the collection of Her Majesty the Queen.

The series of seven tapestry cartoons by Raphael and his studio in the Museum, depicting scenes from the lives of Sts. Peter and Paul, constitute the greatest surviving body of High Renaissance painting outside Italy. The tapestries were intended to be hung in the Sistine Chapel on feast days beneath the 15th-century frescoes by Perugino and others and ultimately beneath the newly frescoed Sistine ceiling, completed by Raphael's arch-rival, Michelangelo, in 1512.

Raphael had already completed some of his most famous work in the Vatican – most notably, *The School of Athens* and *Parnassus* in the Stanza della Segnatura – when Leo X commissioned him to design tapestries for the Sistine Chapel in 1515. The classical style of his maturity was already formed, but it was the first time that he had to compete in the public eye directly with the work of Michelangelo, and he responded with a series of designs of a grandeur appropriate to their size and situation. Of these, *The Miraculous Draught of Fishes* perhaps the most approachable, combining as it does something of the softness and tenderness of his earlier manner, best seen in the marvellously luminous landscape, with the heroism of his figure-style of his last years. The scene is a depiction of the episode from St. Luke (V, 1–10), where Christ miraculously helps the fishermen fill their nets and intimates to St. Peter that he will soon be catching men instead of fish – an allusion to the role of the Papacy, as the successor of St. Peter, in the

cure of souls. The fish and the birds are depicted with a fidelity that enables them to be precisely identified, but probably do not appear simply for their narrative interest and may have a symbolic meaning; for instance, the cranes in the foreground were considered to be symbols of vigilance or safe-keeping in Medieval and Renaissance thought, and the ravens above of heresy or apostasy.

It should be noted that Christ gesticulates with his left hand. This is because the weavers, in making the actual tapestry, cut the cartoon into strips and wove the tapestry from the back looking at the original design below. Thus the finished tapestry is in reverse of the artist's cartoon and Raphael had to allow for this in designing the cartoons. The word 'cartoon' itself has only had a humorous connotation since the 19th century when *Punch* published caricatures of the cartoons for the wall decorations of the new Palace of Westminster. Before that it simply meant a full-scale finished drawing or design immediately preparatory to the final picture or tapestry.

The cartoons came to England when Charles I purchased them for the new tapestry works at Mortlake. They survived the dispersal of his collection under the Commonwealth, being retained for the service of the State, along with Mantegna's *Triumph of Caesar* at Hampton Court. Since 1865 they have been on loan to the Museum from the Royal Collection.   K.H.J.C

Simon Benninck 1483–1561
Netherlandish School
THE MONTH OF MAY, LEAF FROM A CALENDAR OF A BOOK OF
HOURS
Bodycolour on vellum, 14 × 9.5 cm
E.4575–1910. *Salting Bequest.*

Throughout the Middle Ages, Calendars, listing saints' days, month by month, formed an integral part of books for services and for private devotion, such as Psalters and Books of Hours. They were illustrated with the occupations of the months and hence it was in the pages of these religious manuscripts that most medieval pictures of secular activities are to be found. And when, from the late 14th century, there was a renewed interest in direct observation from nature, it was in Calendar illustrations that the early experiments in naturalism were made.

This is a late, exceptionally charming example of the type, dating from about 1540 when the printed book was rapidly replacing the manuscript. It illustrates the month of May with a scene of May Day merrymaking: a boat trip with musicians, a floral procession and dancing in the square. The town appears to be a fantasy, loosely based on Bruges, but all the details of architecture, landscape and figures, down to the unconcerned washerwoman, emphasize the naturalism pioneered by the Flemish School in the 15th century. On the reverse of this sheet is the miniature for April (Courting), another sheet in the Museum has August (Reaping), and September (Sowing, Harrowing) and there are two further leaves from this series in the British Library (MS Add 18855). In these, as in all such Calendar illustrations, there is a striking contrast between the leisure activities, enjoyed principally by the aristocracy, and the work in the fields done by peasants.

Simon Benninck was one of the last major representatives of the early Flemish School. Born in Ghent, he moved to Bruges in 1508 and remained there for most of his life. He worked together with his father, Alexander, on the Grimani Breviary and other important illuminated manuscripts. His self-portrait, painted in body colour on vellum, also in the Museum, epitomizes the close link between the Ghent-Bruges School of Illuminators and the origins of the portrait miniature in Tudor England. Indeed, Simon's daughter Levina Teerlinc (d.1576) was one of the Flemish artists who received official payments for portrait miniatures in the reign of Henry VIII.   C.M.K.

Holbein was born in Augsburg, the son and, eventually, the pupil of a painter of the same name. About 1514 he went to Basle where he was initially principally employed as a designer for printers. He remained in that city, apart from short visits to France and – possibly – Italy, until 1526, when he paid his first visit to England. He remained there until 1528 and painted a number of portraits of courtiers, including the famous group portrait of the More family. On his return to Basle he found that the fanaticism of Protestant extremism severely reduced the amount of work available to him. He returned to England in 1532, remaining there until his death and enjoying royal and court patronage from 1536.

Queen Jane Seymour died in 1537, and in 1539 Thomas Cromwell, then Lord Treasurer and later Earl of Essex, opened negotiations for the King's marriage to Anne, daughter of the Protestant Duke of Cleves, such an alliance appearing politically advantageous. The English ambassador cautiously reported that 'I hear no great praise of her personage, nor of her beauty' and in the Spring of 1539 the King asked for a portrait, but none was forthcoming. In the Summer the King sent Holbein to Duren, near Cologne, to paint Anne's portrait. An oil-painting, now in the Louvre, and the present miniature resulted.

The marriage treaty was signed in September and Anne reached England in December, to be greeted with dismay by her wooer who thought her no better than 'a Flander's mare'. However, the marriage took place in January 1540, to be followed in July by an annulment on the grounds of non-consummation. The political miscalculation cost Cromwell his life at the end of that July, but the ex-queen was well-treated and lived contentedly in England until her death.

Whatever the relationship of the portrait to reality Horace Walpole's high praise of the miniature as 'the most exquisitely perfect of all Holbein's works, as well as in the highest preservation' remains apposite. The ivory box in which the miniature is housed probably dates from the 17th century.

The history of the portrait of 'Mrs Pemberton' is veiled in obscurity. The sitter is traditionally believed to be Elizabeth Throckmorton, wife of Robert Pemberton, although the identification cannot be proved. The arms, dated 1556, which appear on the reverse of the case are Pemberton above Longworth impaling More and appear to relate to a Pemberton-More marriage some fifteen or sixteen years later than the miniature itself, which must be dated to c.1540. The nature of the connection between the portrait and the arms is as yet unexplained. Whatever the identity of the sitter this cool, dispassionate portrait exemplifies (along with the Anne of Cleves portrait) a recent critical comment that 'For Holbein himself scale seems to have been almost a matter of indifference; it was simply a question of what size of image was wanted' and that it 'is as dense and monumental in characterization as any bigger portrait'.

H.B.

Hans Holbein the younger, 1497–1543
German School
ANNE OF CLEVES (1515–1557), FOURTH WIFE OF HENRY VIII,
KING OF ENGLAND
Water-colour, on vellum; in circular turned ivory box in the
form of a rose. Sight size 4.35 cm. Diameter of box 6.1 cm.
Diameter of lid 5.95 cm
P.153–1910. *Salting Bequest.*

Hans Holbein the younger
MRS PEMBERTON
Inscribed in gold ANNO ETATIS SUAE 23
Water-colour, on parchment mounted on part of a playing-
card. At the back, on vellum, is painted the coat of arms of
Pemberton-More, dated 1556. Diameter 5.3 cm
P.40–1935. *Formerly in the Collection of J. Pierpont Morgan.*
Purchased from the Funds of Captain H B Murray's Bequest, together
with donations from Viscount Bearsted and the National Art-Collections
Fund.

Nicholas Hilliard 1547?–1619
British School
A YOUNG MAN LEANING AGAINST A TREE AMONG ROSES
Body colour on vellum, 13.5 × 7.3 cm
P.163–1910. *Salting Bequest.*

Hilliard's *Young Man among Roses* is one of those few images that have, like the *Mona Lisa* or Hokusai's view of Mount Fuji, become a sort of common cultural property, a more potent marker of present concerns than clear document of the civilisation that produced it. Thus, the *Young Man* has been wishfully the image of Mr W H, a wonderful complex summary of the Age of Shakespeare: its embodiment perhaps even if not its only begetter. It is a protean form that might be Sidney or Marlow at one moment, or a free androgynous figment of 20th-century imagination like Orlando, and in that role the aptest manifestation of our Elizabethan fantasies.

We now believe, as it seems on hard rational grounds, that the portrait is of Robert Devereux, 2nd Earl of Essex. As a miniature it fits into an exceptional series of full length works painted by Hilliard between 1585 and 1595, all of first rate court magnates with an interest in commissioning portraits of peculiar splendour, all of them young men who were very close to their sovereign, and the main proponents of her *ethos*. Thus with the portraits of George Clifford, Earl of Cumberland, and Henry Percy the black Earl of Northumberland, we encounter champions of the revived imperialistic chivalry and of the new advanced learning. With Essex himself we see an aspiring champion in both these fields, the friend of Sidney who publicly took on his role after his death at Zutphen. The *Young Man among Roses* shows Essex at this time, arrayed in the Queen's colours of black and white, surrounded by eglantine which was peculiarly her flower, standing by a tree of steadfastness, proclaiming his platonic devotion to her in an emblematic language that was precise yet remains esoteric. The motto – *Dat poenas laudata fides*, literally 'Praised faith gives wounds (or pains)' – may refer to the period when Essex, having covertly married Sidney's widow, was attempting to vindicate his loyalty to the Queen against her displeasure at the match.

There is a scene in Sidney's *Arcadia* where the Virgin Queen is discovered gazing lovesick at a portrait of the young Amphialus, her beloved, as she sits in her coach surrounded by retainers arrayed in her colours. The emblems of the Young Man come exactly from this Arcadian-chivalric background, which was the common culture of the Elizabethan court class, and Essex, commissioning such a portrait of himself, must have had in mind that the Queen would gaze upon it and accept his amends.

J.M.

Nicholas Hilliard 1547?–1619
British School
QUEEN ELIZABETH (1533–1603)
Body colour on vellum on a playing card, 60.3 × 40.8 cm
4404–1857

Queen Elizabeth's reluctance to sit for her portrait is recorded in a draft proclamation of 1563 preserved among the state papers, and the only actual account of a sitting, about the year 1672, is given by Hilliard in his treatise on the *Arte of Limning*. The proclamation was an attempt to control the production of royal portraits by the approval of the work of 'some special person that shall be by her allowed', which was to be a pattern for subsequent portraits by licensed painters. This was however ineffectual in stopping the flood of unauthorized and unworthy images, and culminated in the action of the Privy Council in 1596, who ordered all public officers to assist the Queen's Serjeant Painter in finding and destroying 'unseemly' portraits. From about 1570, the year in which she was excommunicated, the number of official portraits increased to meet the demands of her subjects anxious to prove their abiding loyalty to her and to the Protestant cause. She sat for another portrait circa 1588 when the post Armada series, typified by the Tyrwhitt-Drake painting at Bereleigh, with its background of the naval victory, began to appear.

This miniature portrays the Queen in the last years of her reign, long tresses of her hair falling over her shoulders,

an idealized image, and according to Roy Strong (*Portraits of Queen Elizabeth I*, Oxford, 1963): 'Very close in concept to the "Rainbow" portrait at Hatfield House' and 'making use of the Hilliard "Mask of Youth"'. The Queen may have been wearing a wig at this period, but the story that she was 'as bald as an egg' is almost certainly an invention of a late historian, for curls of her greying hair are preserved at Hatfield House. An interesting contrast can be made between this portrait and an unfinished miniature by Isaac Oliver, (the head a reversed version of the Van de Passe engraving of 1592), a sketch devoid of flattery showing the sunken features of the aged Queen.

The Hilliard miniature is on display in the Primary Galleries, with its original case, the lid of which is of pierced gold, enamelled and set with diamonds and rubies, the back decorated with champleve enamel after a design by Daniel Mignot.

It was purchased by the Museum in 1857, but there is no record of its provenance. J.D.H.

Isaac Oliver d.1617
British School
MINIATURE PORTRAITS OF TWO LITTLE GIRLS
Body colour on card, 5.1 × 3.2 cm
P.145, 146–1910. *Salting Bequest.*

Portraits of infants before the 18th century are very rare, and these two little girls must therefore have been of some great dynastic importance in the English body politic of 1590. At this date miniature painting was still an art restricted to a very narrow circle around the person of the sovereign, a highly educated élite of state officers and courtiers, including their professional advisers and suppliers of cultural services. The portraiture of both Hilliard and Oliver was, as far as we can see, exclusively concerned with this group, and within it, it is usually possible to distinguish by their dress and by the make-up of the portrait the grandees from the professionals. These children were emphatically grandees.

The rarity of strongly individualized child portraits is largely accounted for by the high rates of infant mortality which seems to have inhibited the sort of emotional bonds between parents and their off-spring that seem natural to us. The portrait is a badge of inclusion in a society, proclaiming membership of a household and a place in the wider world. Until children could be relied upon to survive, investment of emotional and material resources in their future seems to have been kept to an economic minimum. The changeover to the modern approach was long drawn out over the 17th and 18th centuries, culminating in the cult of impassioned grief at the death of children recognizable in much 19th-century fiction.

This progresses more or less step by step with the Enlightenment, with advances in practical science and with a broad cultural attentiveness to the mores of marriage and family life. The process, as a phenomenon with real political impetus, begins with the emergence in government of the Protestant rationalist élite under Elizabeth I. The two little girls were presumably scions of this élite, and Oliver, whose work is often distinguishable by the vigorous naturalism of the facial modelling, has endowed each of them with a convincing and characterful presence. The pink and the apple, symbols in Christian iconography of the Virgin and the Fall, are puzzling in this context. They perhaps make some more temporary or anecdotal allusion, reinforcing the personal quality of the images.

The attribution of the miniatures has an amusing history. Male art historians and connoisseurs, possibly influenced by the idea that children were women's business, started the notion that the portraits were by Levina Teerlinc, then a shadowy figure known only from the records of payments to her in the royal accounts. In the 1930s Simone Bergmans, a Belgian scholar, studied the two miniatures and another of similar date which she 'proved' was a self-portrait of Teerlinc. After the war, Carl Winter applied the techniques of style-analysis to the miniatures and argued cogently that they were by Isaac Oliver, and Erna Auerbach seemed to have settled the matter by her discovery that Levina Teerlinc had died in 1576. In ignorance of all this, however, Eleanor Tufts in a book called *Our Hidden Heritage* (New York, 1974) used the miniature to exemplify the theory that male dominated art history had systematically expropriated the achievements of female artists and attributed their greatest works to men. Since then the question has come up every time a new academic course or public exhibition on Women Artists has been planned.   J.M.

Jacques Le Moyne des Morgues 1533–1588
French School
WILD DAFFODIL AND RED ADMIRAL BUTTERFLY
Inscribed *demorgues* and *the admirable Butterfly*
Water-colour and body colours, 27.4 × 18.8 cm
AM.3276a–1856

This is one of the most beautiful of a remarkable series of fifty-nine paintings on thirty-three sheets of flowers, fruits, butterflies and moths, which were painted by a 16th-century artist whose life, both in the New and the Old World, had in its narrow escapes from death, and dramatic vicissitudes of fortune, the quality of an epic adventure story.

Born in Dieppe in 1533, Le Moyne was a Hugenot. In 1564 he was selected as cartographer and artist to accompany an expedition to relieve an earlier settlement of French Hugenots in Florida. His account of the ill starred expedition makes gripping reading. It tells of warring tribes of Indians, mutiny amongst the French camp, of famine, and the providential arrival of the English privateer Sir John Hawkins with supplies. His story culminates in an exciting account of his escape from Fort Carolina during the massacre of the garrison by the Spanish fleet.

On his return to France Le Moyne was commanded by Charles X to lay before him his maps and paintings of the Indians. These pictures (in engraved form) and his story were published after his death by Theodore de Bry in 1591 in *Les Grands Voyages*.

In 1572 Le Moyne made his way to London to avoid the growing hostility to the Hugenots which was to culminate in the Massacre of St. Bartholomew's Day. There he was taken into service by Sir Walter Raleigh, and came to know Sir Philip Sidney, Hakluyt, and the botanist Gervais, author of a famous *Herbal*.

It was in London that Le Moyne published in 1586 his own *La Clef des Champs* illustrated with botanical woodcuts with which the fifty-nine paintings in the Victoria and Albert Museum are closely connected. He died at Blackfriars two years later in 1588.

The Victoria and Albert Museum's water-colours by Le Moyne are outstanding botanical illustrations, remarkable for their directness and truth to nature. But ironically they were initially acquired in 1856 as one of the first purchases of the Museum, almost by accident, and solely because they were bound up in an extremely fine French late-16th-century brown calf binding. Since the discovery of the importance of the water-colours in 1922, they have been mounted separately, and can be studied in the Print Room.   L.L.

46

The admirable Butterfly

A.M. 3267.ᵉ '56.   demorgues   V. A. M.

Denis Van Alsloot active 1599–d. before 1628
Flemish School
THE TRIUMPH OF THE ARCHDUCHESS ISABELLA IN THE
BRUSSELS OMMEGANCK OF SUNDAY, 31ST MAY 1615
Signed and dated lower left *Denis V A* (in monogram) *Alsloot A⁰
1615* Numbered *449* and inscribed *La Cincquiesme*
Oil on canvas, 117 × 381 cm
5928–1859

This great procession (or *Ommeganck*) was held annually in
Brussels to commemorate the translation centuries earlier of a
miraculous image of the Virgin from Antwerp to a church in
Brussels. In 1615 an especially splendid show was provided to
honour the able and popular Archduchess Isabella (1556–1633),
daughter of Philp II of Spain and sovereign of the Spanish
Netherlands, who in that year was Queen of the Fete.

To record the occasion the archduchess commissioned six
paintings from Denis van Alsloot, depicting the entire
procession (rather old-fashioned by contemporary Florentine
standards) passing through the Grande Place, plus two copies
of two of the canvases. The latter remain in Brussels, but only
four of the original six subjects survive, two being in the Prado
at Madrid and two in the Victoria and Albert Museum.

The Museum's paintings were bought at different dates in the 19th century (1859 and 1885) having been alienated at some time from the Spanish Royal Collections.

The painting illustrated is the most important in the series, depicting as it does the ten pageant cars which formed the most spectacular element in the show, which was basically a procession of the city's clergy and magistrates with the members of the fifty-four trade guilds. Much else of interest is recorded in Alsloot's paintings, but the major significance of this canvas, the fifth, lies in the representation of the cars. There are ten altogether and in the order of procession (i.e. from the front rank facing left to the upper right corner of the picture) they are as follows: (1) the Car of King Psapho (who traditionally taught parrots to speak of his glory); (2) the Car

of the Court of Isabella (with a 'stand-in' for the archduchess); (3) the Car of Diana and her Nymphs; (4) the Car of Apollo and the Nine Muses; (5) the Car of the Stem of Jesse (the family tree of Jesus Christ); (6) the Car of the Annunciation; (7) the Car of the Nativity; (8) the Car showing Christ among the Doctors; (9) the Car of the Virtues of Isabella; and (10) the Car representing the Ship of the Emperor Charles V (first used at the Emperor's funeral ceremonies in Brussels in 1558 and continually re-used).

Apart from the interest of the pageant itself Alsloot, the super-realist, has exactly caught the citizenry of Brussels in their holiday finery watching and participating in a particular moment in their city's history. H.B.

Louis Le Nain 1593–1648
French School
LANDSCAPE WITH FIGURES (LA HALTE DU CAVALIER)
Oil on canvas, 54.6 × 67.3 cm
CAI.208. *Ionides Bequest.*

Born at Laon in eastern France, Louis was the second of three brothers – the others were Antoine and Mathieu – who shared a studio in Paris from about 1630 and painted genre scenes with a realism unusual in French art of the period. The name of Louis became attached to the best of their paintings, but as there are no securely documented works and the signed ones only bear the name LE NAIN, the traditional differentiation between the styles of the three brothers was decisively rejected in the retrospective exhibition of their work held in Paris in 1979. Even so, the paintings ascribed to Louis form a distinct group and it is as well to retain the original names for the sake of convenience.

The figures are silhouetted against a low sky and a flat agricultural landscape. They were painted over the completed landscape, of which the green shows through their clothes. The rare beauty of the picture lies in the monumental quality of each individual figure. They do not appear to relate to each other, but they have statuesque proportions and are imbued with human dignity. In this respect Le Nain's peasantry differ from those of his Netherlandish contemporaries, which tend to be boorish and clownish, to be laughed at or to be looked down upon, rather than admired. The V&A painting is very similar to other exterior genre groups of like size and equally cool tonality, such as the *Charrette* in the Louvre. This is signed *Le Nain 1641* and hence our picture may reasonably be dated to about the same period. Another version was owned by Picasso and passed with his collection to the Louvre.

The Le Nain scenes of rural life remain highly unusual in French painting until similar subjects were once again explored by 19th-century painters such as Millet. This has raised the question: for whom were they painted? It has been suggested that they found patrons among the growing section of the urban middle class which invested in land in the 17th century at a time when the French peasantry was economically hard pressed. There is evidence that much land was bought for the purpose of investment rather than residence, and it has been suggested that the *cavalier*, whose status is indicated by the ownership of a horse, represents the class of *fermier* who managed the estate of an absentee landlord. Such speculation is hardly susceptible to proof, but there is no doubt that these rare scenes of French peasant life are social documents as well as monumental figure studies.   C.M.K.

This plate shows miniatures from the hundred or so years between the death of Nicholas Hilliard and that of Peter Cross. In that period the art of limning made one of those loops that occur quite frequently in history, from a fairly strict adherence to the technical practices of Hilliard, through an exuberant experimentalism in style and materials, and back to a consciously 'Tudor' style of hard linearism and flat blue background. Thus John Hoskins, who inherited the mantle of Hilliard in the service of James I, must have learnt from his predecessor the manner epitomized in the *Unknown Woman*. Hilliard recommended publicly this even lighting and concentrated attention to the mobile features of eye and mouth to catch the 'witty smilings and stolen glances'. On the other hand, he was secretive in the *Treatise* about how jewels should be painted to give the literally three-dimensional effect of his richest presentations. The fact that Hoskins used in this miniature the authentic Hilliard technique of dropping coloured molten resin on to the surface with burnished grains of gold and silver, is prima facie evidence of a direct relationship between older and younger master.

Hoskins, like Hilliard, seems to have worked almost exclusively for the close circle round the sovereign, and he was at his busiest in the 1630s, the decade of the Caroline absolutism, when his output was absorbed in spreading the ethos of Royalism in its prime van Dyckian mode. For Samuel Cooper, the limner's functional attachment to the court led to the special crisis of the early 1640s when the King fled from his capital: what was Cooper to do? He stayed in London, and began grappling with the problem, both practical and philosophical, of painting men such as Cromwell whose fundamentalist reading of the Bible seemed to forbid image-making. One of the achievements of the Wars and Inter-Regnum was accordingly the invention of a portrait iconography that was, warts and all, a moralistic address to the minimal corporeal reality of the sitter, a form of strict descriptive discourse as acceptable to the militant puritan as to the tolerant rationalist of the later 17th century. In the Restoration Cooper's finest work was in this vein, in the series of sketch studies of members of the court élite including almost certainly this portrait of the King's favourite sister Henrietta.

John Hoskins c.1590–1664/5
UNKNOWN WOMAN
On vellum, 5.5 × 4.3 cm
Signed JH in monogram
P.32–1941. *Gift of Mrs E Joseph.*

Samuel Cooper ?1608–1672
SIR WILLIAM PALMER
On vellum, 5.7 × 4.5 cm
Signed and dated SC 1657
P.3–1956. *Purchased with funds from R H Stephenson Bequest.*

Samuel Cooper ?1608–1672
HENRIETTA DUCHESS OF ORLEANS
On vellum, 7.2 × 5.5 cm
Inscribed by the artist with sitter's name
P.110–1910. *Bequeathed by George Salting.*

Peter Cross c.1645–1724
ROBERT KERR, 4TH EARL OF LOTHIAN
On vellum, 7.6 × 6.5 cm
Inscribed, signed and dated 1667
P.5–1982. *Purchased partly with funds from the R H Stephenson Bequest.*

Thomas Flatman 1637–1688
SELF PORTRAIT
On vellum, 6.8 × 5.5 cm
Signed and dated 1673
P.79–1938. *Gift of the Basil Long Memorial Fund.*

The adaptation of such a closely observed style to the re-established conventions of court portraiture was a marked trend in Cooper's late finished work, developed further by his immediate successors Nicholas Dixon and Peter Cross.
The most interesting and the most rigorous however of those who built on the aesthetic principles that had appeared in the 1650s was Thomas Flatman. His *Self Portrait* is an extreme example of the art of portraiture used like the protestant conscience for self examination, and is analogous to Rembrandt's later self portraits especially in using the medium with rough refusal to disguise or blend away the paint strokes.

Bernard Lens 1682–1740
Richard Whitmore aged about 3,
On ivory, 7.6 × 6.3 cm
Signed and dated 1718
P.13–1971. *Purchased.*

Bernard Lens 1682–1740
Katherine Whitmore aged about 2
On ivory, 7.6 × 6.3 cm
Signed and dated 1724
P.14–1971. *Purchased.*

It was this main line of the limning tradition that finally re-established itself in the 18th century, the tradition being renewed and purified by the diverse antiquarianism of Lens on the one hand and Horace Walpole on the other. Lens seems to have reacted partly against the technical elaboration of enamel painting and partly against the increasing softness and smokey, flattering indistinctness of the late Peter Cross. His portraits of the Whitmore children, hard in silhouette and brightly coloured in the clear light of day, seem to look back to the 1590s, and in particular to the two little girls of Isaac Oliver.

J.M.

Johannes Goedart 1617/20–1668
Dutch School
A VIEW IN THE ISLAND OF WALCHEREN, WITH THE CASTLE OF
WESTHOVEN AND THE CHURCH TOWER OF MIDDELBURG
Signed *Joh. Koedaert*
Oil on oak panel, 30 × 41 cm
557–1882. *John Jones Bequest.*

Largely because of the enthusiasm among early 19th-century collectors and artists for works of the Dutch school, England remains the best place outside Holland to find new master-pieces of the great century of Dutch culture. Attention, however, is often focused on the leaders – van Goyen, the Ruisdaels, Hobbema – and the doubtful or unsigned works tend to be classified around their styles. Presumably the *oeuvre* in oils of Goedaert has thus been distributed away from him: only four paintings are now known, all signed.

His name is of greater eminence in the history of natural science, and he seems to have been a member of a group of intellectuals in the mid-17th century active at Middelburg in the comprehensive study of the laws of nature. Goedart's own field was the morphology of insects, and his approach was classically empirical, the close study and record of appearances through all the changes of the life cycle. His great work, the *Metamorphosis Naturalis . . .* (Middelburg, 1662–9) was illustrated with engravings after his own coloured drawings, executed from the life during years of breeding and study of insect forms. Those habits of visual study and the skills of accurate record were fundamental to the 'scientific' revolution of the 17th century.

What is often overlooked by aesthetic critics of art is the status of landscape painting similarly as a descriptive study of the natural environment. The image of Walcheren may not be a study in the sense applicable to the Insects, but landscapes, especially in this highly detailed and almost naturalistic idiom, had a special significance in the world view of the natural philosophers. Hung only in those public parts of the house assigned by convention to them, paintings of people, places and things belonged to and helped to establish the sense of intellectual order, the types and hierarchies, that comprised the Creation. Thus *A View in the Island of Walcheren*, hung in a Middelburg house, would have located the town in its wider environment and placed the doings of man in nature, representing them in a house that would itself be a microcosm of the greater world outside.   J.M.

57

Jean François de Troy 1679–1752
French School
THE ALARM, OR LA GOUVERNANTE FIDÈLE
Signed and dated indistinctly at the bottom of the fountain
J.F. de Troy 1723
Oil on canvas, 69.5 × 63.8 cm
518–1882. *Jones Bequest.*

This characteristic example of the art of the French *Régence* was painted in the last year of the regency of Philippe Duc d'Orléans (1674–1723), the nephew of Louis XIV, who was Regent of France from 1715 during the minority of Louis XV, great-grandson of Louis XIV.

It is usual to regard the *Régence* as a period in art-history extending from c.1705 to 1730 and marking the transition in France from the Baroque to the Rococo, with an easily identifiable character of its own. The Regency was marked by a relaxation in social behaviour, partly engendered by the profligacy of the Regent himself and partly a reaction against the constraints of the later years of Louis XIV. An erotic element appeared in much contemporary art and whilst this canvas is in no sense scandalous it clearly provided a mild element of titillation to the original spectator with its implication of sexual intrigue. Verses which appear on an engraved version of this subject – such engravings being very popular – makes it clear that the faithful *gouvernante* is not in fact warning of the approach of a father or jealous lover but rather of the dangers inherent in too receptive a response to the young man's protestations of love.

58

De Troy achieved eminence as a painter of genre, mythological, historical and religious subjects, as a portraitist and as a designer of tapestries. He became an *académicien* in 1708 and died in Rome as director of the French Academy there. It was for his lighthearted so-called *tableaux de modes* – suggested by the earlier success of Watteau – that he became most celebrated in his lifetime. These canvases were painted specifically to illustrate the costumes and manners of an increasingly frivolous society and, apart from their intrinsic merits, now constitute splendid records of the age. An early biographer comments that De Troy was himself something of a fribble and much in favour with 'respectable but tender-hearted ladies of the Paris bourgeoisie'. He undoubtedly painted his elegant scenes of contemporary life for a new clientele, many of his patrons being newly prosperous bankers and financiers. It is recorded that he painted no less than thirty-two overdoors for one such client!

The new elegance, lightness, fluidity of line and freshness of colour exemplified in De Troy's work met with a ready and enthusiastic response in a society reacting against staidness and formality in public behaviour.

H.B.

Nicolas Lançret 1690–1743
French School
THE SWING (L'ESCARPOLETTE)
Oil on canvas, 70 × 89 cm
515–1882. *Jones Collection.*

An attempt was made in 1908 by Sir Claude Phillips, to attribute this picture to Watteau. It is now generally ascribed to Lancret, but it may be in part the work of a studio assistant. This was common practice with painters who received many commissions. Probably only the faces and figures, together with the finer details of the modelling, are from Lancret's own hand. Nevertheless, this is iconographically a more interesting picture than *Le Berger Indecis* (No.547–1882, Jones Collection) which is indisputably by Lancret himself.

Lancret was an imitator of Watteau, painting *fetes galantes* and *Commedia dell'Arte* scenes that were, in their time, as successful as the master's: a contemporary report, 1723, described him as 'the pupil of the late M. Gillot and the rival of the late M. Watteau'. His elegant and lively compositions lack those qualities of melancholy and psychological insight so characteristic of Watteau, but substitute humour and naturalism. Here he has chosen a subject that would have been familiar to the pleasure-loving court of Louis XV, a scene of amorous dalliance (the *fete galante* itself was a new subject in painting, an art of the manners and morals of love). The swing, in such a context, was a recurrent motif in 18th-century painting – Lancret himself repeated the subject at least eight times. As well as suggesting leisure, idleness and passivity – for the swinger's action is controlled by her companion – it carried a weight of erotic connotation and innuendo. The constant back and forth motion could suggest inconstancy or fickleness, but was also a specific erotic metaphor for the physical act of love.

The picture was cleaned in 1964, revealing a decorative framework on all four sides. This indicated that it had originally been a decorative panel transformed into an easel picture by over-painting at a later date. The nature of the picture's original purpose is one reason to suppose the composition partly or wholly the work of an assistant.

Though the colour and the handling are not equal to Lancret's best work, it is nevertheless a charming and competent picture. The landscape setting is depicted with a convincing naturalism, and is not simply a painted backdrop to the action. The delicate colouring is typical of Lancret, as is the evident skill in rendering rich fabrics. The boy's costume is in the style of the period, but the girl's attire is essentially fancy dress. The simple 'shepherdess' gown is again derived from the theatrical fantasies of Watteau. The picture is a Rococo confection, most evocative of the frivolity and hedonism which constitute the public image of court life.   G.M.S.

Francis Hayman RA 1708–1776
MAY DAY
Oil on canvas, 138.4 × 240 cm
P.12–1947. *Bought with the aid of a contribution from the National Art-Collections Fund.*

The cheerful scene depicted here was, until the early 19th century, one of the well-known sights of May Day in London. The milkmaids, who delivered their milk to houses, danced before their customers' doors dressed in their best clothes and accompanied by a 'garland' or cloth-covered frame hung with flowers and silver vessels hired from a silversmith. The garland was carried by one or two porters or by the milkmaid herself. Competing for attention, and donations, were the boy chimneysweeps, making a loud and discordant noise with their brushes and shovels. The figures have been put into an imaginery half-Italianate rural setting appropriate both for the season and for the original placing of the painting, an open-air supper-box at Vauxhall Gardens, also known as New Spring Garden.

By the time of Rowlandson's visit the gardens were already 123 years old, but it was not until after 1728, with a new lease by Jonathan Tyers, that they came to great fame as a setting for musical and other events. 'The hint of this rational and elegant entertainment' was said by a contemporary to have come from Hogarth, and it is certainly true that some of the decorations were the work of his artist friends who met at Slaughter's Coffee house in St. Martin's Lane and at his Academy nearby. Most notable was the series of forty-eight large paintings (5 feet by 8 feet), completed by 1744, which adorned the supper-boxes, the majority of which were painted by Hogarth's boon companion Frank Hayman or his assistants. They formed, in effect, the first public art gallery in England, and although not on the highest level as work of art, being broadly painted and essentially ephemeral, their impact was considerable. The Gentleman's Magazine noted in 1755 that they had all been retouched because of damage from 'those curious connoisseurs, who could not be satisfied without *feeling* whether the figures were alive'.

The naturalism and modern subjects of the paintings, drawn from popular literature or everyday life, formed the greatest possible contrast with the Baroque allegory of previous public art. Their style was generally a combination of Hogarth's direct observation of life and the elegant naturalism of Hubert Gravelot, the French draughtsman and teacher, who was in London between 1733 and 1746. He greatly influenced the St. Martin's Lane group, notably Gainsborough, whose early work shares a number of characteristics with that of Hayman. Of the 15 or so surviving Vauxhall paintings, *May Day* is the least damaged, and the one which best preserves Hayman's touch. The slightly Italianate mood is enhanced by his favourite device of contrasting deep shade with fitful reflected light.

Also in the Museum are the Vauxhall paintings *Sliding on the Ice* and a fragment of *The Wapping Landlady*, by Hayman and his assistants.

M.S.

Arthur Devis 1711–1787
British School
THE DUET 1749
Signed on stretcher of harpsichord *Artr Devis fe, 1749*
Oil on canvas, 115.6 × 103.5 cm
P.31–1955

In England during the 1720s a new kind of portrait painting became popular: the 'conversation piece'. This was more intimate and informal than the conventional portrait, and the figures much less than life-size, often set back in space as if on a stage. The sitters were usually a family group seen in the privacy of their own park or country house, and the scene was often enlivened by some kind of narrative incident or social activity. This form of group portrait was derived from Dutch 17th-century interior views, and those 'conversations' set in parks and gardens had their origins in the *fetes galantes* of Watteau and his followers in France.

Arthur Devis, of Preston, Lancashire, was a master of this minor genre. Most of his contemporaries – Hogarth, Zoffany, Hayman, Mercier – painted some conversation pieces. but almost every one of Devis's 281 known works are small full-length portraits. In most cases the sitters have been identified, but here we have an anonymous couple, the lady seated at the harpsichord, her companion, who has just laid down his violin, handing her a sheet of music. There is a greater degree of intimacy and communication between the sitters here than is usual with Devis: perhaps it is for this reason that the picture has also been known as *The Love Song*. The musical device was commonly used in painting as a symbol for love and harmony.

This canvas, which is set in a remarkably fine contemporary frame carved and gilded in the English Rococo style, is typical of Devis's work of this period. The couple are shown in a large sparsely furnished room dominated by the view of the park through the tall Palladian window. The Italianate view paintings on the walls proclaim their fashionable taste and suggest that they have travelled on the Continent. The skilful handling of landscape and perspective, and the sophisticated rendering of colour and texture in the costume are surprising in view of the stiff and rather awkward posture of the doll-like figures. Devis had trained with the Dutch topographical painter Peter Tillemans (1684–1734): consequently he was competent with landscape and architecture, but had no experience of life drawing. This difficulty was exacerbated by his use of a wooden dummy as a substitute for the sitter when at work in the studio.

Though he moved to London in 1742, Devis seems not to have felt the influence of the liveliness and naturalism then being introduced from France. The animation and informality of the Rococo were clearly incompatible with his painstaking, though elegant, compositions. His provincial and self-consciously naive style looks back to Tudor and Jacobean portraits where costume, gesture and attributes are symbols of status. Likeness and personality are secondary to this theme.   G.M.S.

Samuel Scott 1702?–1772
British School
A THAMES WHARF
Oil on canvas, 159.7 × 135.2 cm
FA.249

Bought for the Museum in a London saleroom in 1865 as a work by Peter Monamy and Hogarth this painting remained attributed to Monamy until 1949, although the Hogarth attribution was abandoned at an early stage. There is now no reason to doubt that it is the work of Samuel Scott and another version of the subject, long attributed to Scott, hangs in the hall of the London Fishmongers' Company.

Scott, like Monamy, began his career as a marine painter, not turning to the topographical scenes which earned him the nickname of 'the English Canaletto' until fairly late in his career, that is to say after the arrival of Canaletto in England in 1746 and that artist's speedy demonstration of the existence of a ready market for such subjects.

This work appears to date from the 1750s and vividly depicts how London's maritime trade was handled at the many riverside wharves and quays. The identification of the location of this scene has long been a problem which will probably remain insoluble. When bought the painting was entitled 'The Old East India Wharf at London Bridge', while the version at Fishmongers' Hall has been traditionally entitled 'Custom

House Quay'. Another possible location which has been suggested is Bear Quay, which was next to London Bridge. All these seem to be unlikely, however, and it may well be that the scene is, in fact, a sort of *capriccio* or else should be located much further down river, possibly at Shadwell (where the East India Company had a warehouse), or at Deptford, or at Blackwall where the large East Indiamen customarily moored. The large bale in the right foreground is marked V.E.I.C. which does suggest the possibility of some connection with the East India Company. The ship moored at the left, however, is a two-decker man-of-war flying a commodore's flag.

Much interesting detail is included in the picture, most notably, perhaps, the tread-mill crane which is housed under the penthouse at the right. The figures of the men at work and in conversation about the quay have something of the liveliness and spontaneity found in the figure-painting of Luca Carlevaris, Canaletto's Venetian precursor in topographical painting. The spaniel seated in the foreground is thought to be possibly the work of Sawrey Gilpin (1733–1807), the animal painter, who became Scott's pupil in 1749.   H.B.

66

67

François Boucher 1703–1710
French School
MADAME DE POMPADOUR (1721–64), MISTRESS OF LOUIS XV
Signed and dated *f. Boucher 1758* on stone lower right
Oil on canvas, 52.4 × 57.8 cm
487–1882. *Jones Bequest*.

After the flight of her father from Paris in 1725 in consequence of a black market scandal, Jeanne Antoinette Poisson was brought up by Le Normant de Tournehem, a director of the French East India Company and principal collector of taxes. In 1741 de Tournehem married Antoinette to his nephew Le Normant d'Etioles; four years later she became the King's mistress and was created Marquise de Pompadour. Even though there was a formal physical separation in 1750, Madame de Pompadour retained a position of central importance at the Court and remained a formidable patron of the arts in her own right.

Boucher knew her when she was still Madame d'Etioles, as he belonged to a group of artists assembled at the house of Le Normant de Tournehem, and he benefited greatly from her patronage when she became Madame de Pompadour. Although he is best known as a painter of decorative figure subjects,

whose portraits are few and far between, he painted her portrait at least seven times – there are fine versions in the Wallace Collection and in the Scottish National Gallery, Edinburgh. He also decorated her theatre in 1746, her dining room at Fontainebleau in 1748 and her chateau at Bellevue two years later.

In spite of the emphasis on the sumptuous satin and courtly splendour of the dress, this portrait surprises by its freshness and directness. In this way it is in strong contrast to the society portraits of a decade or two later when dress, wigs and make-up had become markedly more ostentatious and sitters' bearing ever haughtier. The background of trees and roses, also, although in a somewhat artificial convention, retains sufficient naturalism to remind one that Boucher had spent years as a young man drawing landscape from nature.   C.M.K.

Thomas Gainsborough RA 1727–1788
British School
THE PAINTER'S TWO DAUGHTERS
Oil on canvas, two canvases joined, 40.7 × 61.6 cm
F.9. *Forster Bequest.*

Gainsborough always held that likeness 'was the principal beauty and intention of a Portrait', but in his depictions of his daughters Mary (born c.1748) and Margaret (born c.1752), the likeness is endued with a special quality of intimacy and understanding. He loved to paint 'Molly' and 'The Captain', as he affectionately called them, and there survive today five double as well as several single portraits of the girls at various ages. Doubtless their attraction for him as sitters was the greater because they were not patrons with exigent demands, but his own children upon whom he could practice his skills as a portraitist with freedom to experiment in a spontaneous and informal manner.

It is not known exactly when Gainsborough executed this double portrait, but it was probably in 1758, when his daughters would have been about ten and six years old. It appears that the girl on the spectator's left is the elder, and she is therefore taken to be Mary, who later married the celebrated oboe player, Johann Fischer. As in all the other double portraits, the girls are shown in close sisterly contact with each other; here they are linked by Mary's arm stretching up to rest on Margaret's hair. (The girls' hair would have been cut in this short style to fit neatly under mob caps.) Margaret, under the restraining hand, turns to face us with an

almost haughty gaze, an expression very similar to one she wears in the slightly later portrait now in the National Gallery, *The Painter's Daughters holding a Cat.*

The two heads are modelled with great delicacy, the artist tracing the contours with a meticulous hatching technique, his brush charged with luminous colour. This contrasts with his free treatment of the nebulous leafy background.

The history of the painting is somewhat obscure, but according to tradition, it passed from Margaret Gainsborough to John Jackson, RA, and was then divided vertically into two halves, one going to W C Macready, the actor, and the other to John Forster, the friend and biographer of Dickens. Forster, as is recorded, ultimately acquired Macready's portion which he reunited with his own, the joined painting coming to the Museum in 1876. Closer examination does however suggest that the work may actually have begun life as two individual portraits: the backgrounds of the two halves do not entirely tally, and Mary's left arm seems out of alignment with the rest of her torso, the upper arm being over-painted to connect with the raised forearm on the right hand side of the painting. If this is so, it would help to explain the portrait's division between two previous owners.

M.W.T.

James Barry 1741–1806
British School
SELF PORTRAIT
Oil on paper, 42 × 34.4 cm
564–1870

In his fourth discourse, Sir Joshua Reynolds states that 'History painting and sculpture should be the main views of any people desirous of gaining honours by the Arts. These are the texts by which the national character will be judged in the after ages.' Barry's uncompromising adherence to this doctrine and his vehement criticism of those who fell short in this matter was eventually to lead to his expulsion from the Royal Academy in 1799.

We see him here, on the evidence of his apparent age, during, or just after the completion of his greatest work; the cycle of oils commissioned by the Society for the Encouragement of Arts, Manufactures and Commerce in 1777 to decorate their rooms in the Adelphi. Each of these massive paintings – the largest being 12 feet by 43 feet – symbolizes a crucial episode in the attainment of 'human culture'. It is only in the context of this series and of Barry's relationship with his contemporaries at the Academy that we can fully understand this depiction of himself.

In one panel of the cycle he uses his own portrait as that of the classical Greek artist Timanthes. Though not a study for Timanthes, the present portrait is certainly a closely related work. Within the Adelphi cycle Barry subtly deflects meaning away from a celebration of the achievements of the society, towards a declaration of the artist's central role in the process of civilization. Such an act exemplifies his conception of the primary function of his profession and makes clear his identification of himself as the chief civilizing influence, and by extension, 'saviour', in Britain at the time. When seen in the light of his quarrelsome relationship with the Academy,

this observation allows us to make a distinction between the abstracted look that traditionally signifies intellectual concerns in contemporary self-portraiture and Barry's pensive expression here – clearly we are looking to the face of a martyr.

Barry's attitude to portraiture is often misunderstood. Though a less elevated genre than History, it was certainly of the second order, and thus not beneath his interest. However, artists who specialized in portraits, he believed, could not attempt History, for they were 'incapable of studying the entire man, body and mind'; nevertheless, a History painter could 'occasionally confine himself to any part of his subject (i.e. the face) and carry a meaning, a dignity and a propriety into his work that a mere portrait painter must be a stranger to.' In these ideas he is consistent with general European History theory, which not only considered the human figure as art's most expressive vehicle, but in the study of physiognomy as codified by Le Brun, considered facial expression capable of embodying man's intellect and soul.

Barry depicts himself here perhaps contemplating not only his recent hardships in painting the Adelphi *gratis*, but also in a wider sense the project's demonstration of the fundamentally untenable position of the British painter of History.
His resultant posture as martyred saviour helps explain his importance for historians of Romanticism; for in this role his classicism can be connected to the cult of melancholy and alienation that was later to surround the Romantic philosopher Jean Jacques Rousseau.   C.P.T.

Jonathan Skelton c.1735–1759
British School
VIEW OF ROME, WITH THE TIBER, THE CASTLE OF S. ANGELO,
AND, IN THE BACKGROUND, ST. PETER'S
Inscribed on the back with title and date *May 1758*
Water-colour, 37 × 53 cm
P.11–1925

Although Skelton was one of the first English artists to visit
Rome, the English taste for Italian views was already strong
and landscapes by Claude Lorraine, Gaspar Poussin and their
followers had begun to feature prominently in many British
collections. The Grand Tour, including a visit to Italy, played
an essential part in the upbringing of many young Englishman
of rank and fortune, and this led to a demand for topographical
views of the monuments and more prominent buildings of
Rome. Skelton, one of the earliest English artists to work
exclusively in the water-colour medium, hoped to gain
commissions for such views, of which this is an outstanding
example. But his hopes were dashed by ill health, and the
calumny that he had Jacobite sympathies damaged his
opportunities to show his works to visiting English aristocrats.

Little is known of Skelton's life in England, not even the place
or date of his birth, but from 1754 to 1757, according to
inscriptions on drawings he was working mostly in South
London and Kent. In 1757 he left for Italy, and his letters from
Rome, which he reached in January, 1758, have an immediacy
which brings before the reader the crowded artist's cafes of the
city, the difficulties he faced through being suspected of being
a Jacobite spy, and the problems of living on the allowance
made by his patron, to whom he wrote; 'The purse you lent
me that looked so round and plump when it left Croydon was
reduced the beginning of this week to a mere Skeleton, it often
made my Heart ake to see it.' The letters are printed in
Volume XXXVI of the Walpole Society, 1956–8.   L.L.

74

Paul Sandby 1730–1809
British School
WINDSOR CASTLE: THE NORTH TERRACE LOOKING WEST
Body colour, 38 × 53.5 cm
D.1832–1904

Paul Sandby has been called, erroneously, the 'father of English water-colour'. In fact water-colour was a well-established method, which Sandby's skills, practised over a long career, promoted and elevated. He was a founder member of the Royal Academy and this position enabled him to raise the water-colour to exhibition status.

Sandby's earliest landscapes were produced for a military survey in the Highlands. This fostered an accurate and detailed approach. In 1752 he joined his brother Thomas, who was Deputy Ranger of Windsor Forest, in schemes of landscaping and improvement. Windsor Castle and its environs were to be a major source of Sandby's subject matter for the next twenty years. These studies combine topographical accuracy with a feeling for the Picturesque.

This view is a very late version dating from about 1800, of an earlier subject. The original was painted sometime in 1770, and appeared as an aquatint in Sandby's publication *Five Views of Windsor Castle and Eton*, 1776–7. Although he makes a

concession to the passage of time by minor changes of costume, the figures themselves, and the architecture, are drawn from his old sketchbooks. The soldier seated on the parapet also appears in a drawing in the Royal Collection of the gardens at Old Somerset House. Sandby was a master of the dramatic composition, a device which raised his 'real views from nature' above mere topography. Here the picture is divided diagonally – the dark mass of the castle apartments, and the shadowed expanse of the terrace oppose a vast area of clear evening sky above the flat landscape of the Thames valley.

Sandby was unusual amongst the 18th-century English water-colourists in that he used body colour (or gouache) for a large part of his output. This medium, in which the water-colour is mixed with white to make it opaque, was popular on the Continent. Sandby used pure water-colour for his military work and for subjects intended for the engravers, but he favoured body colour because it was better suited to the necessarily large scale of his exhibition works.　G.M.S.

Francis Towne 1740–1816
British School
THE SOURCE OF THE ARVEIRON: MONT BLANC IN THE
BACKGROUND, 1781
Signed and dated *F. Towne. delt 1781*. Numbered *No. 53*.
Inscribed in ink by the artist on the back of the original mount
LIGHT FROM THE RIGHT HAND NO. 53 THE SOURCE OF THE
ARVIRON (*sic*) WITH THE PART OF MOUNT BLANC DRAWN BY
FRANCIS TOWNE SEPT. 17TH 1781
Pen and ink and water-colour, 42.5 × 31.1 cm (on four sheets
joined)
P.20–1921

Francis Towne was probably the most original artist working
in the water-colour medium in the 18th century. He regarded
himself, nevertheless, as primarily a landscape painter in oil
and deeply resented a dismissive contemporary description of
himself as 'a provincial drawing-master'. His water-colours
were virtually unknown for a century after his death, most
having remained with him until bequeathed to friends and
thus remaining in private collections, apart from his Italian
drawings which – as he desired – were given to the British
Museum.

Although trained in London with his life-long friend William
Pars, his roots lay in Devonshire and he spent the major part
of his working life in Exeter, although he exhibited regularly in
London and frequently spent long periods there. He was
apparently a diffident and unworldly man who was satisfied to
cultivate his Devonshire friends and patrons.

It seems likely that he originally used water-colour as an aid in
the development of his oil compositions, but by 1777 he was
using the medium characteristically, albeit still somewhat
tentatively, to record impressions of a tour in Wales.
The turning-point of his career as a water-colourist came in
1780, when he paid a visit to his friend Pars in Rome and in
the course of his stay there considerably developed his
technique. The present drawing belongs to the remarkable
series of majestic studies of Alpine scenery made by Towne on
his journey home through Switzerland in September 1781.
Towne's view owes nothing to the 'Gothick' romanticism of
Horace Walpole and his friends thirty years earlier.
He banishes all extraneous 'picturesque' elements such as
wayside shrines and ruined bridges. His vision is of the
greatest severity and his presentation austere in the extreme.
He achieves the expression of his fascination with the
geometry of Nature by the most economical means, reducing
everything to the simplest terms and achieving a noble
monumentality by his skilful arrangement and lighting of
inter-reacting planes. This subject reveals Towne's preoccupation with outline and pattern in the highest degree as
well as his subtle use of delicate washes to achieve his desired
ends.

In due course, with the advent of the vision of Cézanne and of
the Cubists a century after his death, Towne's vision became
more widely comprehensible and there is now due appreciation
of the originality of his contribution.   H.B.

John Robert Cozens 1752–1797
British School
THE TWO GREAT TEMPLES AT PAESTUM
Water-colour, 24.5 × 37.2 cm
Inscribed on back in artist's hand: *Temples of Pestum Executed for William Beckford*
P.2–1973

Nearly all of Cozens's water-colours can be linked with one or other of his two continental journeys. *The two great Temples at Paestum* derives from his second tour, that of 1782 in the employ of his patron William Beckford, and is one of ninety-four that Cozens made for Beckford on their return to London in 1783. Beckford's presence in Italy seems to have been impelled not by scholarly considerations but by a desire to experience once more the sensations of his first steps on classical soil, those recorded in *Dreams, Waking Thoughts, and Incidents* (1782). This introspective literary work went far beyond the accepted formula of topography and history to which conventional travelogues were composed. He begins: 'Shall I tell you my dreams? To give an account of my time is doing, I assure you, but little better' and it was perhaps Cozens's ability to embody this oneiric melancholy that first recommended him to Beckford.

Like their literary counterpart, Cozens's series of water-colours are desultory evocations of mood rather than a methodical visual record of the tour. Thus *Paestum* differs greatly from the conventional views to be seen in contemporary topographical prints; Cozens chooses to depict the temples from the south-east, looking out to sea. In doing so he avoids the visual confusion of the surrounding mountains and the huts of the tourist site. Paestum had been 'discovered' in the 1760s and was popular as an example of 'the state of Grecian architecture in its infancy'. To the right is visible the temple of Neptune, to the left the so called Basilica.

The high viewpoint may have been achieved by making the drawing from the city walls, though it is probable that Cozens raised the eye level artificially in order to achieve the visual pattern created by the punctuation of the columns by the horizon. The resulting configuration works both to impress us with a strong sense of the temples as structures raised from the vast debris-strewn plain, and, by showing them as skeletons – reminders of the long-expired civilization that erected them – as *memento mori*.

Yet, although the emotion is enhanced by the historical association, its potency depends less on the architecture or the banditti, than on the quality of light – the still evocation of sunset. Here Cozens had to rely on memory alone, for the sketch of the subject (Hamilton sketchbooks, vol.4, no.12) does not note the 'effect' by either wash or word. It is precisely this intermediate mental process – a combination of imagination and memory – that gives the painting its tonal unity and simplicity, and by way of these its power to affect us. Unlike Piranesi who had made views at Paestum four years previously, Cozens expresses here the delicate and poignant rather than the powerful and imposing, relying on quiet desolation to move us in contemplation of our own fate.   C.P.T.

80

Thomas Gainsborough 1727–1788
British School
TRANSPARENCY: COTTAGE AND POND, MOONLIGHT
Oil on glass, 28 × 33.6 cm
P.33–1955. *Bequeathed by E E Cook through the NACF.*

In 1781 Gainsborough's friend Philip de Loutherbourg
astonished London by the display of his *Eidophusikon,* or
Representation of Nature. This elaborate contrivance, consisted of
a six-foot wide stage with brilliant lamps, slips of stained glass,
trees made from cork and moss, mechanical models, transparencies and sound effects which were all employed to
produce moving scenic effects. On one occasion Gainsborough
was helping to produce the sound effect of a thunder storm by
shaking a sheet of copper, when a real thunder storm broke
out. De Loutherbourg gripped Gainsborough by the arm,
and said 'Our thunder is better, by God!'.

Gainsborough's experience in helping with this apparatus,
and his knowledge of contemporary stained glass painting,
inspired him to produce a set of ten, or possibly twelve,
transparencies, one of which is reproduced here. They were
viewed in a peep-show 'show-box', illuminated from behind by
four small candles and seen through a lens. The light was
diffused and varied by a coloured silk screen inserted between
the candles and the glass, so that remarkable flickering effects
of light were produced.

A painting on opaque canvas can only achieve a luminance
scale of 20 to 1, but by painting on glass a far greater
approximation can be achieved to the luminance scale of nature
which can reach 760 to 1 on a bright sunny day. Gainsborough
enjoyed experimenting with the wider range of tonal effects
available by using a glass support as can be seen in this
moonlit nocturn with its dramatically lighted cottage door and
windows, a characteristic picturesque subject. Some of the
other transparencies relate closely to oil paintings by
Gainsborough, and it seems probable that he painted many
more than these surviving examples, experimenting with
similar compositions both on glass and canvas.   L.L.

Thomas Rowlandson 1756–1827
British School
VAUXHALL GARDENS
Pen and ink and water-colour, 48.2 × 74.8 cm
P.13–1967. *Bought with the aid of a contribution from the National Art-Collections Fund.*

James Boswell described Vauxhall Gardens as 'a place of elegant and innocent entertainment peculiarly adapted to the taste of the English nation, there being a mixture of curious shew – gay exhibition – musick, vocal and instrumental, not too refined for the general ear; for all of which only a shilling is paid'. Small wonder that Rowlandson, a keen observer of human behaviour, was a habitué, finding as his friend Henry Angelo records, 'plenty of employment for his pencil'.

Vauxhall Gardens was Rowlandson's first major attempt at an elaborate group composition, and it is a tour-de-force including more than fifty potentially recognizable figures. The scene is an alfresco concert at Vauxhall, with the singer Mrs Weichsel, accompanied by a group of musicians, entertaining the audience from the Orchestra, where performances were held in fine weather. Below them are the supper-boxes, the figures in the left-hand box once (but no longer) thought to be Dr Johnson and his party. Some of the other *dramatis personae* are more readily acceptable as contemporary portraits. The two ladies holding court under the central tree are said to be the beautiful Duchess of Devonshire and her sister Lady Duncannon, and among their entourage are plausibly identified Captain Topham, gossip writer to The *World* and 'Macaroni of the Day', who quizzes them through a glass; Admiral Paisley, with eye patch and wooden leg; and, to the right of the tree,

James Perry, editor of the *Morning Chronicle*, in Highland dress. The focal point of the main group under the trees is supposedly 'Perdita' Robinson whispering with her lover, the Prince of Wales.

This genre of painting, reflecting the habits and tastes of a sophisticated society at play, was not new, but in the disposition of this fashionable assemblage Rowlandson combines a flair for dramatic grouping with a caricaturist's eye for telling incident. The dominant verticals of the trees and Orchestra building provide an imposing framework in which to weave a rhythmic profusion of episodic and decorative detail. His highly calligraphic cursive style gives the drawing a feeling of spontaneity, as though it were a work of on-the-spot reportage, and the colours too are washed on with extreme fluency and clarity.

It is ironic that although this water-colour is one of Rowlandson's most famous and influential works, there is no record of its existence from its exhibition at the Royal Academy in 1784 until its subsequent re-appearance in a small country shop in 1945, the image being disseminated solely through the faithful aquatint made after it by R.Pollard and F.Jukes in 1785. A smaller version of the painting, with variations, is now in the Paul Mellon Collection.   M.W.T.

84

George Morland 1763–1804
British School
THE RECKONING
Oil on canvas, 73.6 × 99 cm
FA.237. *Given by F Peel Round.*

George Morland was the most popular painter of picturesque rustic genre scenes in 18th-century England. His output was prodigious. The more drunken and profligate his life became, the more paintings left his easel to placate creditors.
He preferred to sell his work through an agent, although this was unusual for the time and altered the nature of patronage for future artists. *The Reckoning*, however, was a private commission for Peel Round's grandfather, who took the work wet from Morland's easel. Therefore, unlike so many of his paintings it was never engraved.

The Reckoning combines Morland's affection for the labouring classes with a pertinent observation of 18th-century social manners. The scene takes place in a publican's stable. There the pot boy of the inn is asking a farmer to make payment for the services he has received. At first the picture appears straightforward but then one notices the disgruntled expression on the farmer's face as he digs his hand reluctantly into his front-fore breeches. It appears that the pot boy has

been too hasty in asking for money. The ostler who is watching the boy and farmer has not fastened the girth strap round the grey cob's belly. The two bull mastiffs and the casual onlooker loitering in the doorway reinforce this moment of action by drawing the viewer's eye to the dialogue between the central group. However, there is a feeling of ambiguity as to the nature and tone of their conversation; this ambiguity is prevalent in many of Morland's works.

The Reckoning also shows Morland's passion for painting animals. The grey cob, mastiffs and springer spaniel are treated with great care and attention to detail. The two mastiffs have those anthropomorphic qualities that became the trademark of Sir Edwin Landseer during the Victorian era. Morland tapped the national consciousness with his enthusiasm for horses and dogs and re-inforced the view of his upper-class patrons that the English countryside was a pastoral Arcadia of well-kept yeomen and peasants.   A.N.

Henry Fuseli 1741–1825
British School
THE FIRE KING, C.1801–10
Oil on canvas, 99 × 124 cm
158–1885

Fuseli's subject is taken from Sir Walter Scott's poem 'The Fire King' of 1801. A Crusader, Count Albert, has been captured by his Infidel enemies and has fallen in love with the Sultan's daughter, Zulema. To gain her hand he has to abjure Christianity, fight his former allies and pass three nights deep in a cavern 'Where burns evermore the mystical flame which the Curdmans adore'. The first two vigils are uneventful. Here we see Count Albert on the third, during which the Fire King appears 'borne on the blast' to give the Crusader a magical sword to use against the Christians. His coming causes volcanic eruptions which terrify Count Albert:

> 'High bristled his hair, his heart flutter'd and beat,
> And he turned him five steps, half resolved to retreat . . . .
> I ween the stout heart of Count Albert was tame
> When he saw in his terrors the Monarch of Flame'

Fuseli came to London from Zurich in 1764. His immediate contacts were in literary circles, though in 1768 Reynolds was sufficiently impressed with his drawings to urge him to study in Italy and become a painter. He remained eight years in Rome, during which time he sent back paintings for exhibition at the Royal Academy. His experience there of Michelangelo, of the Antique, and to some extent the Mannerist styles of Parmigianino and Rosso profoundly affected him and form the basis of his subsequent style. In his subject matter however, he is completely individual, searching diverse literary sources for dramatic and frequently supernatural events.

It is Fuseli's ideas on expression that differentiate him from his contemporaries at the Royal Academy. Although, like them, he considered the human form to be the prime expressive vehicle – landscape plays little part in his work – and although both parties agreed that classical art supplied the exemplar to which they must strive, for Fuseli the academic appreciation of Antiquity was too limited in esteeming beauty at the expense of all else. Beauty in Fuseli is subordinated to expression – without expression he says '[Beauty] fades into insipidity, and, like possession cloys'. In this he parallels the German literary movement *Sturm und Drang* (Storm and Stress), in which Shakespeare is preferred to Racine and spontaneity of emotion opposes convention and decorum.

Count Albert's terror is used by Fuseli as a means of inducing sublime emotions in the spectator. As Burke had written in his *A Philosophical Enquiry into the Origin of Our Ideas of the Sublime and Beautiful*, terror is one of the most affective emotions of the sublime. Ghosts and apparitions Burke considered as stimuli that most powerfully affect the mind. In this connection Fuseli was contemptuous of Academicians who 'Whenever they venture from their lumber rooms of heraldry and drapery into the field of fancy expose themselves with conceits of impotent puerility. With the apparition of the Fire King then, Fuseli demonstrates his own ability in the invention of supernatural characters, for as William Duff had written in 1767, it is in this class that 'the highest efforts and the most pregnant proofs of original Genius' are to be found.

C.P.T.

William Blake 1757–1827
British School
SATAN AROUSING THE REBEL ANGELS 1808
Signed *W. Blake 1808* in lower left hand corner
Water-colour, 51.8 × 39.3 cm
FA.697

Nathless he so endured, till on the beach
Of that inflamed sea he stood, and called

His legions, angel forms, who lay entranced
Thick as autumnal leaves that strew the brooks
In Vallambrosa . . .

Paradise Lost Book 1 299–303

Satan Arousing the Rebel Angels is one of twelve illustrations to
John Milton's *Paradise Lost*. The set was commissioned by
Thomas Butts, Blake's major patron of the 1800s. In depicting
scenes from Milton, Blake was following a well-worn tradition;
among his contemporaries, Fuseli, James Barry and Thomas
Stothard had all done so.

This particular subject was considered the most popular from
Milton's epic, and Blake produced several versions. The Butts
Satan, with its dominant full frontal figure, raised above the
writhing forms of the fallen angels, all contained within a small
picture area, has a precedent in Thomas Lawrence's work of
the same subject exhibited at the Royal Academy in 1799.

Whilst closely following the same compositional formula as his
predecessors, Blake broke with tradition by evolving a highly
personal and complex interpretation of Satan's rise and fall
which was potentially in conflict with the spirit of Milton's
poem. In the initial books of *Paradise Lost* Satan is a figure of
terror and power: 'He called so loud, that all the hollow deep
of Hell resounded'. This force is not suggested in Blake's
water-colour. Blake's Satan has an Apollonian beauty as he
tries to raise the seven enchained angels, hardly the legions
'thick as autumnal leaves' that Milton writes of.

Satan's pose is also reminiscent of *Glad Day*, the first engraving
Blake did in 1780. This raised nude figure with outstretched
arms recurs repeatedly in Blake's work. In this instance,
such familiarity with the pose tends to diminish the expressive
potential necessary in depicting a truly Miltonic Satan.   A.N.

Thomas Girtin 1775–1802
British School
KIRKSTALL ABBEY, YORKSHIRE: EVENING, C.1800/01
Water-colour, 31.8 × 52 cm
405–1885

Although Girtin is known to have made water-colours *in situ*, while before the subject, his usual practice was initially only to make pencil drawings in a pocket sketchbook and later work up these compositions in the studio. *Kirkstall Abbey* is clearly of this last kind. Not only do we have the evidence of its size to support this, but also the finished nature of its execution and sustained power of imaginative force.

In the summer months of 1800 Girtin was touring in Yorkshire, staying for a time as the guest of his patron Edward Lascelles at Harewood. *Kirkstall* probably derives from sketches made during this tour, perhaps being worked up that winter on his return to London.

Girtin's subject matter is consistently topographical, and always depicts specific places. However, the present picture demonstrates the crucial change in his expressive aims that distinguishes his late work from the topographic tradition. Whereas formerly his approach had concentrated on the fabric of the building, here we find a new interest in atmospheric effects that are intended to heighten our melancholia in apprehending the scene. Approaching sunset shadows everything in autumnal browns inducing a pensive mood, and the tower, conceived as a ruin dramatically silhouetted against heavy cloud, by careful choice of angle, is reduced to one wall that frames an area of mellow evening sky. In achieving this dramatic configuration Girtin has not been

over-concerned with topographical accuracy, rather his concentration has been upon an evocation of his own emotional responses. Thus, although we are viewing from the south, he depicts the low light of the setting sun as emanating from behind the tower; in reality it would be shining from the direction indicated by the east-west axis of the nave. Moreover, the belfry window has been enlarged – he gives it an extra sixth light. Enclosing delicate tracery resembling that of an east window, the tower now seems to have a transient fragility not present in the actual sturdy structure.

By including contemporary incident – the strollers and their dog, a haystack and smoke from the part of the ruin that had by then been converted into a farmhouse – we are invited to contrast the present with the medieval past, in so doing perhaps reflecting upon mortality:

> 'The great projecter of these haughty piles,
> With all his riches, honours and renoun,
> Hides his poor head in dust – and is no more!'

(Lines addressed to a Company of Young Persons, whilst viewing the Ruins of Kirkstall Abbey, C Cayley, c.1798)

Girtin was to make one further water-colour of the Abbey (J H Mayne, *Girtin*, pl.4), a closer view of 1802. He died in November that year aged 27.   C.P.T.

93

John Sell Cotman (1782–1842)
British School
CHIRK AQUEDUCT
Water-colour, 31.6 × 23.2 cm
115–1892

Chirk Aqueduct is one of the most beautiful of English water-colours. Its quality derives from the simplicity of its composition, three great arches of an aqueduct standing alone in the countryside, and the delicate play of washes that envelop it and suggest the fall of sunlight on the scene. Cotman was of the same artistic generation as Turner and Girtin, and like them sought to make landscape-water-colours that are not simply portrayals of a place but make an appeal to our emotions. It was his apprenticeship with Girtin that taught him to use wash to suggest subtle changes of tonality and atmosphere, and his membership of Girtin's sketching club 'The Brothers' that helped to develop his sense of the underlying significance of a theme.

Chirk Aqueduct is a fine example of their approach to a subject. The aqueduct must have been quite new when Cotman sketched it, on one of his tours of Wales in 1800 or 1802. Cotman does not show us the whole structure, but takes us up to its piers to suggest its size and dominance over the surrounding landscape. It is shown off-centre, to suggest a progression of arches to the left and right, and its dominance is further reinforced by its reflection in the stream below. The sun beats down and cuts great dark diagonals of shade out of its arches to give us a sense of the building's height and massiveness, and its strength and powers of endurance are contrasted with the fragility of the rickety wooden fence glimpsed through the arches below. All detail that would give us a specific sense of place is omitted, and the surrounding trees and foliage of the hills are reduced to an undifferentiated green mass which serves as a backdrop to the new building.

Recent studies have in fact suggested that this is not a real place but an imaginary structure of the artist's own invention. However, Cotman must surely have stood under a similar structure in order to produce so convincing a water-colour. It is a record of a powerful emotional experience rather than a description of a place, and is the painted equivalent of a poem or an ode by Keats. It was this development of the poetic and atmospheric qualities of the landscape that brought British landscape-painting to pre-eminence in the early 19th century and remains our greatest contribution to European painting.

K.H.J.C.

94

John Smart c.1742–1811
British School
MISS HARRIET AND MISS ELIZABETH BINNEY
Signed and dated *John Smart pinxt 1806*
Water-colour, oval 22.3 × 24.2 cm
P.20–1978

The miniature portrait enjoyed a revival during the later 18th century; it did not, however, regain its former status as a court art. There were still aristocratic patrons, but also many new clients amongst the wealthy middle class. John Smart, one of the outstanding miniaturists of the period, found most of his sitters amongst the ranks of the military and colonial classes.

This double portrait is exceptional in several respects. It is unusually large for a miniature. In this it reflects its date: by the 19th century the miniature was no longer designed as a keepsake or piece of jewellery to be worn by the owner. Miniature painting was simply another form of portraiture, and its practitioners began to adapt their techniques and format to compete with the conventional wall-hung portrait in oils. The large size probably explains why this picture was painted on card, and not on the ivory base which was more commonly used for miniatures. However it had always been Smart's practice to make preliminary drawings on paper so he was well able to adapt his techniques. Instead of the usual head and shoulders view, the two girls, seated at the harpsichord, are shown three-quarter length.

This is a remarkably sophisticated portrait for Smart whose work was usually simple and direct, focusing on the personality of the sitter and avoiding elaborate costume or accessories. He has used the lateral oval skilfully, making a positive virtue of the empty spaces. The curves of the girls' arms, and their shallow décolletages echo the shape of the frame. The cool restrained Neo-Classicism of colour and style is in keeping with the fashionable costume and elaborate Empire-style hair ornament of the sitters. A typical feature in Smart, each girl smiles slightly. The whole is very finely detailed, with brilliant handling of flesh and fabric. The water-colour is applied in the soft stippled manner characteristic of Smart.

In fact Smart's style changed very little through his career: works of the 1760s bear all the hall-marks of his maturity. This was perhaps due to his modest and isolated practice. He spent ten years in India from 1785, painting members of the British community, and the household of the Nawab of Arcot. He painted Charles Binney, Secretary to the Nawab, in 1797, after Binney's return to London. This gentleman was obviously well-pleased with the result, and commissioned this portrait of his daughters Harriet (on the left) and Elizabeth (right) in 1806.

G.M.S.

Jean-Baptiste Isabey 1767–1855
French School
NAPOLEON FRANÇOIS JOSEPH CHARLES BONAPARTE, DUKE OF
REICHSTADT (1811–1832), SON OF THE EMPEROR NAPOLEON I
Signed *Isabey* on wheelbarrow to left
Water-colour on ivory (head and shoulders): set within an oak
panel over which is stretched paper on which the remainder of
the composition is painted in water – and body colour, overall
size 26.1 × 30.3 cm, head and shoulders 8.2 × 7.6 cm
P.40–1948. *Formerly in the Collection of J Pierpont Morgan.*
Bequeathed by Sir Bernard Eckstein, Bart.

This delightful portrait of the pathetic son of Napoleon and his second wife, the Hapsburg Archduchess Marie-Louise, shows him playing in a garden, probably at the Palace of Schönbrunn, after the abdication of his father in 1814 and the withdrawal of his mother to her native Austria in April of that year. It has been justly described as 'perhaps the most moving of Isabey's works'.

The child, styled King of Rome at his birth, was briefly recognized as Napoleon II during the Hundred Days, but after his mother's return to Vienna she made no attempt to press her son's succession rights in France. From 1815 he was known only as Prince of Parma (by right of his mother's title to that duchy) until his grandfather, the Emperor Franz I, on the advice of Metternich, created his Duke of Reichstadt in July 1818, granting him precedence *after* the Austrian archdukes with the minor style of Serene (rather than Imperial) Highness. Napoleon was thus safely converted into an Austrian duke and was educated as such.

Despite physical frailty he desperately wanted to be a professional soldier until an inherent weakness of the chest asserted itself and he died of consumption at Schönbrunn on 22 July 1832 aged only twenty-one. He was buried with his Hapsburg ancestors in the Imperial Crypt in Vienna from whence his remains were removed to Paris on the orders of Hitler in 1940 to join those of his father in the Invalides.

Isabey (a pupil of the miniaturist Dumont and of David) was a portraitist favoured by Queen Marie-Antoinette who managed to survive the Revolution and the Terror to become eventually a court painter to Napoleon I. Isabey's friendship with the Empress Josephine served to ensure his success which, almost incredibly, continued with Josephine's successor, Marie-Louise, whose teacher he became. Soon after the fall of the Empire came the death of the former Empress Josephine and Isabey, without immediate patrons in Paris, arranged to travel to Vienna in the suite of Talleyrand in order to paint the eminent personages assembled for the Congress of 1815. It is most likely that this engaging work was painted during that visit.

Isabey's representation of the little prince in his toy uniform, with toy sword, sabretache and drum, playing with an ivory cup and ball against a fluently sketched background of trees, disregarded emblems of horticulture lying to the left, is a lively evocation of happy childhood games for which – given the ambiguity of the boy's situation and the frustration of his short life – the spectator can only be grateful.   H.B.

James Ward 1769–1859
British School
BULLS FIGHTING, WITH A VIEW OF ST. DONATT'S CASTLE,
GLAMORGAN
Oil on panel, 132 × 228 cm
220–1871

In 1803 Sir George Beaumont, patron, artist and collector,
and virtually the founder of the National Gallery, was given by
his wife Sir Peter Paul Rubens's landscape *The Chateau de Steen,
Autumn*, now in the National Gallery. It was taken to the
studio of the President of the Royal Academy, Benjamin West,
who invited, among others, James Ward, the animal painter,
to see it. Ward determined to produce a painting which would
rival Rubens, and used a panel of almost exactly the same size
to paint *Bulls Fighting*. When it was completed some critics,
amongst them West and Beaumont, admired it, others, notably
John Constable, dismissed it as being a mere imitation of an old
master.

In reality Ward's painting is far from being a mere imitation of
Rubens, for the bulls are inspired by a work by George Stubbs.
It is interesting to see how Ward has changed the classical,
static calm of Stubbs' composition into the fulcrum for a
romantic synthesis of moods — a struggle which mirrors the
threat of coming storm, and the high winds which have
uprooted the massive tree, the central element of the design.
All these factors give the picture, not the tranquil enjoyment
of Rubens' landscape, with its Shakespearean feeling for the
ordered cycle of the seasons, but an emotive Wordsworthian
identification with the wilder aspects of nature. Like Rubens'
own copies after Titian, Ward's painting can be enjoyed both
as an expression of its own time, and as a vivid lesson in art
historical appreciation.   L.L.

John Crome 1768–1821
British School
VIEW ON MOUSEHOLD HEATH, NEAR NORWICH
Oil on canvas, 54.5 × 81.2 cm
232–1879

Mousehold Heath is situated about one mile to the north east
of Norwich town centre. In Crome's day it was still unsur-
rounded by modern suburbs, and was a favourite place for
artists to paint and sketch; Cotman painted a water-colour of
the scene that is now in the Castle Museum at Norwich.
The Norwich school of painters was the most lively and
talented of all local societies of painters that flourished in
England in the early 19th century. Crome was its undisputed
leader, having been a founding member of the Norwich Society
of Artists in 1803.

View on Mousehold Heath may be the picture that Crome
exhibited at the Norwich Society in 1812 as *Boy Keeping Sheep:
Morning.* Crome shows us a shepherd boy on a hillock of the
heath silhouetted against the sky with his dog and his sheep
below him. The vastness of the heath is glimpsed through a
crack in the low-lying ground on the right. Such a mundane
subject is Dutch in inspiration, but the colours are clear and
bright and painted in broad bands of colour that suggest the
influence of Richard Wilson, then one of the most respected
painters amongst innovative landscape-painters of the early
19th century. The composition may be based on a plate from
Gainsborough's *English Scenery*, etched by W F Wells and
published in 1803–4.

In a famous letter to his pupil James Stark in 1816, Crome gave
some account of the principles that governed his art. A painter
should aim at breadth of handling and avoid details, 'forming
one grand plan of light and shade, this must always please a
good eye and keep the attention of the spectator and give
delight to every one. Trifles in Nature must be overlooked
that we may have our feelings raised by seeing the whole
picture at a glance, not knowing how or why we are so
charmed.' In his fluid handling of the paint Crome has
produced a picture that is not so much of a shepherd-boy and
his sheep as of infinite light and space.   K.H.J.C.

John Constable 1776–1837
British School
FLATFORD MILL FROM A LOCK ON THE STOUR
Oil on canvas, 24.8 × 29.8 cm
135–1888. *Gift of Isabel Constable.*

The Victoria and Albert Museum owns the largest collection of Constable's work in the world; most of it derives directly from his studio and was given by his daughter Isabel in 1888. Many of the pictures in this gift are small oil-sketches and studies of nature, painted out-of-doors, a technique which Constable seems to have used more than any other artist of his time. By sketching directly from nature in oils Constable was able to capture the spontaneity of natural effects that would have been lost if he had composed his pictures solely from drawings.

Flatford Mill from a Lock on the Stour dates from about 1811. By then Constable had decided on the course he had to follow if he were to fulfil his desire to be a 'natural painter'. The picture portrays the scene at one of his father's mills on the river Stour, this one at Flatford, the others being at Dedham, and Stratford all in the heart of 'Constable country' in Suffolk. Constable generally restricted himself to landscapes of places he knew well, perhaps because he found them less distracting to the real subject-matter of his paintings, the effects of climate and weather on the interaction of sky, trees, foliage, water and man. No preliminary studies survive for this scene, and it is likely that Constable simply set up his easel on the lock and painted what he saw before him. He has used a canvas prepared with a warm reddish ground to act as a tonal background to his colours, which are applied in great

thick brush-strokes whose energy is barely contained by the rigid diagonals of the composition. The swirling brush-strokes in the sky suggest the movement of clouds, and gives them an almost physical tangibility which matches that of the clump of trees in the background. This sympathetic use of paint to suggest texture is mirrored in his portrayal of the river, where small horizontal brush-strokes glide into one another and suggest the flow of the river and the play of light on moving water. No single thing or object is precisely defined; the picture is not so much a portrayal of a particular place as a study of the weather at a particular time. No wonder the painter Fuseli said; 'I like the landscapes of Constable . . . but they make me call for my greatcoat and umbrella.'

This small study was the basis for a large painting of the scene, probably exhibited at the Royal Academy in 1812 and recently rediscovered in America. Constable's sense of composition was sufficiently developed by this time for an unplanned sketch to become the basis of an exhibited painting, and shows how his study of Claude and the Dutch School of landscape-painters had not atrophied his vision but given him the artistic confidence to work where and how he pleased. These small oil-sketches may also owe something to the example of Rubens, who also produced large paintings direct from sketches and whose landscapes have a similar rough overall texture.

K.H.J.C.

John Constable 1776–1837
British School
BOAT-BUILDING NEAR FLATFORD MILL
Oil on canvas, 50.8 × 61.6 cm
FA.37. *Sheepshanks Gift.*

Boat-building near Flatford Mill is a particularly important work in Constable's oeuvre. Exhibited at the Royal Academy in 1815, it sums up those aspects of his art that Constable considered to be most important at a time when he was actively canvassing support to be elected an Associate of the Royal Academy. Its purpose was to gain recognition for his art in established artistic circles.

The scene is a pleasant summer's day on the banks of the river Stour. A barge is being constructed in Constable's father's boatyard by the mill to carry his flour down the river to Mistley in Essex on its way to London. The unfinished boat is shown with a degree of detail unusual for Constable, but it is not painted with any more care than the surrounding trees. The general effect is of a placid, tranquil and uneventful day.

As *'Boat-building'* was so important to Constable he took special trouble over its creation. The composition was carefully worked out in a pencil drawing in his sketchbook of 1814 in the museum and we know that he was advized to study the work of Claude before embarking on the picture in order to attain the correct degree of 'finish' that would make it acceptable to members of the Academy. We also know that he painted the picture almost entirely out-of-doors. According to David Lucas, the engraver of Constable's sketches, Constable

knew when to finish a day's work by the smoke that arose from a neighbouring cottage when supper was cooked.
The picture thus achieves a remarkable degree of verisimilitude to the visual sensation of a late summer afternoon in the country. The eye is not called upon to focus on the boat alone; it can explore the fields in the distance or investigate the clumps of foliage in the shadows on the right of the picture. The overall consistency of light and shade in the scene has not been equalled until the advent of the French Impressionists.

Sad to relate, Constable was unsuccessful in his attempt to be elected to the Academy. It was not until 1819, when his contemporary Turner had been a full member for seventeen years, that he was elected an Associate.

It is worth remembering that Constable's pictures often depict some kind of industrial or agricultural activity by the river Stour. Those who see Constable's pictures as images of rural calm should remember that the river Stour was navigable and Constable's father's mills formed part of the industrial activity that took place on its banks. Constable's concern for accurately reproducing the day-to-day business of the countryside is such that he has been called an 'industrial landscape painter' as opposed to a purely rural landscape painter.   K.H.J.C.

John Constable 1776–1837
British School
STUDY OF TREE TRUNKS
Oil on paper, 24.8 × 29.2 cm
323–1888. *Gift of Isabel Constable.*

In 1819 the scale of Constable's exhibition pictures changed. In that year he exhibited the first of his 'six-footers' at the Royal Academy, the 'White Horse' in the Frick Collection in New York. These large pictures were intended to bring his art to public attention and take their place in the history of landscape painting as the natural successors to Hobbema, Van Ruisdael and Rubens. He went to enormous trouble in their execution, even to the extent of painting full-scale sketches for some of them. The Victoria and Albert Museum owns two of these sketches, for the *Hay-Wain* of 1821 (National Gallery) and the *Leaping Horse* of 1825 (Royal Academy). The success of Constable's exhibition pictures may be gauged from the fact that he was elected an associate of the Royal Academy in November of 1819 and that the *Hay-Wain* has since become the most famous landscape in the history of British painting.

This emphasis on careful finish and composition in Constable's exhibition pictures contrasts with the increasing informality and broad handling of his out-of-door sketches. Often they focus on some hitherto neglected aspect of the landscape or some transitory effect of atmosphere or weather. This study of tree trunks is thought to date from 1821, when Constable was making his cloud studies on Hampstead Heath. It is no more than the fragment of a scene, a study of the way in which sunlight filters through the leaves of a tree and illuminates its trunk. The leaves are painted with a yellow that suggests the brilliance of the sun and the tree trunk is painted in broad, smooth strokes that blend into one another and suggest the sheen on the bark of the tree in the light of the sun.

The composition is deliberately oblique, with the trees rising up on the left and the grass bank sloping down on the right, which leads the spectator's eye out to the right of the composition, where a girl is portrayed in a few brush-strokes in the sun at the bottom of the bank. Constable has depicted a sensation that everyone who has walked in the countryside will know, that of coming out of a dark wood or bank of trees into the sunlight beyond.

It may seem odd that Constable's sketches out-of-doors should grow looser in handling and composition when his exhibition pictures show a much higher degree of finish and attention to composition based on a study of the old masters. However, it was all the more important to Constable to keep up his study of nature in order to handle the elements of these large pictures naturalistically. He was in effect keeping close to the source of his art, as he himself summed it up to his biographer Leslie: 'My limited and abstracted art is to be found under every hedge and in every lane, and therefore nobody thinks it worth picking up.'

K.H.J.C.

John Constable 1776–1837
British School
STUDY OF CLOUDS AND TREES
Oil on paper, 24.8 × 29.8 cm
162–1888. *Gift of Isabel Constable.*

Constable's interest in landscape painting was a deeply felt response to the beauty and variety of nature. 'Painting is with me but another word for feeling' he told his friend John Fisher. Yet he saw the process by which he translated his vision into two dimensions as essentially scientific. 'In such an age as this', he wrote, 'painting should be understood, not looked on with blind wonder, nor considered only as a poetic aspiration, but as a pursuit, legitimate, scientific and mechanical.'

The most striking example of his 'scientific' analysis of nature is the group of cloud studies that he executed at Hampstead in the years 1821–2. They depict the sky at a particular moment in time, and under certain weather conditions, just as a portrait-painter might try and capture some fleeting but particularly characteristic expression on a sitter's face. Often these studies are annotated with precise details of the time and weather conditions in which they were painted.
The immediate stimulus to this group of cloud studies may have been the work of the meteorologist Luke Howard, whose two volumes on 'The Climate of London' were published in 1818–20. They contained a reprint of his paper of 1802 'On the Modifications of Clouds' in which he divided cloud formations into three categories that are still used today; cirrus, cumulus, and stratus. Constable certainly knew of these categories, since

he owned a copy of Thomas Forster's 'Researches about Atmospheric Phenomena' in which they are described, and moreover one of his cloud studies in the museum (No.784–1888) seems to be inscribed with the word 'cirrus'. However, Constable's cloud studies should not be seen simply as illustrations of these categories, but as parallel investigations of his own. He is particularly concerned to show not just the appearance of the sky at any particular moment, but its effect on the scene and the way in which other objects on the sky-line, such as the trees, respond to it. For Constable the landscape was an organic unity, no part of which could be studied in isolation from another.

Constable's aim in producing these studies was to improve his understanding of a hitherto neglected part of the landscape, the sky, which he felt had an expressive value of its own. He told Fisher that he had often been advised to consider the sky as 'a white sheet drawn behind the objects' but for him it was 'the standard of scale and the chief organ of sentiment in a landscape. These studies were not intended for any particular landscape by Constable, but the understanding of the structure of the sky that he gained from them was put to good use in the dramatic backgrounds of *Hadleigh Castle* (1829) and *Salisbury Cathedral from the Meadows* (1831) of his later years.   K.H.J.C.

John Constable 1776–1837
British School
BRIGHTON BEACH, WITH COLLIERS
Oil on paper, 14.9 × 24.8 cm
591–1888. *Gift of Isabel Constable.*

Brighton Beach, with colliers dates from 1824. In that year Constable paid the first of a number of visits to the newly fashionable town for the sake of the health of his wife, Maria, who was dying of consumption. He was little taken with the town, whose crowded beach he described as 'Piccadilly by the sea-side', but could not fail to be impressed by the clarity and immensity of the sea and the sky there and their appearance in the sun and the wind. He made a number of sketches there, some of which he sent to his friend John Fisher for inspection.

This study is precisely annotated and dated by Constable '3d tide receding left the beach wet – Head of the Chain Pier Beach Brighton July 9 Evg., 1824 – My dear Maria's Birthday Your God-daughter [Constable's daughter Maria Louisa was Fisher's god-daughter] – Very lovely Evening – looking Eastward – cliffs and light off a dark grey [?] effect – background – very white and golden light.' Constable thus portrayed the scene with the same kind of atmospheric accuracy with which he painted his cloud studies. As it is evening the beach is almost deserted, and the study is a simple portrayal of the three elements of sand, sea and sky. Each element has its own almost geometric segment of the composition and the sand and the sea are portrayed with a thick impasto which suggests the undulations of the sand and the movement of the waves. The colours are bright and lucid and the dark band of damp sand is clearly visible. The whole is painted on a light pinkish ground to suggest the clarity of evening light at the sea-side.

The portrayal of colliers (coal-ships) may seem slightly unusual in a popular sea-side resort like Brighton, but probably reflects Constable's concern to show the landscape as a place in which people live and work. Artistically they provide a much-needed central accent of black which links the three zones of colour together. Constable purposely avoided a 'picturesque' depiction of the scene, with fishing-boats, nets and fishermen, as 'these subjects are so hackneyed in the (Royal Academy) Exhibition, and are in fact so little capable of that beautiful sentiment that landscape is capable of.' Instead he portrays the brightness and breeziness of the scene on a light summer's evening.

Fisher was delighted with the sketches, which he described as 'full of vigour, and nature, fresh, original, warm from observation of nature, hasty, unpolished, untouched afterwards.' In portraying the sea-shore as a consciously modern scene in the sunlight and the wind Constable has rejected the former traditions of sea-scape painting and looks ahead to the work of Boudin and the Impressionists in France in the latter part of the century.

K.H.J.C.

Francis Danby 1793–1861
British School
DISAPPOINTED LOVE
Exhibited RA 1821
Oil on panel, 60.5 × 111 cm
FA.65. *Sheepshanks Gift.*

Danby studied at the Dublin Society of Arts and under the landscape painter James O'Connor. In 1813, he visited London and decided to settle in Bristol where he married. This rich town presumably offered a market for his work, and its lovely valleys and woods provided inspiration. An informal society of art lovers, amateurs and professionals met here for sketching and summer trips to the Avon Gorge and elsewhere. Danby's landscape style developed into a realistic, intimate view of nature in which contemporary figures play a natural role – probably due to his contact with the sketching society. The early works are simple views; later he introduced mood and genre, influenced by the Bristol artists Edward Bird and E V Rippingille.

Danby was ambitious to establish himself as an English painter and his exhibition works were carefully contrived to impress. His second exhibition work *Disappointed Love* (Royal Academy, 1821) created a stir. It shows a young woman in white set against a dark background, distraught and weeping into her lap on a secluded river bank. The clues to her 'disappointed love' lie strewn about her: her bonnet and shawl, a miniature of a young man, an open wallet with a letter and torn scraps of paper. The Redgraves in *A Century of British Painters* (1866) assumed that she was about to take her own life.

This striking painting works at both narrative and poetic levels. The highlighting of the figure against a dark background adds to the drama of the scene. That Danby was aware

of the possibilities of light and shade can be seen from other Bristol landscapes; probably this was due to Turner's influence. Symbolism is used to reinforce the story: the girl's white dress refers to her innocence, while the unnaturally large, drooping plants, overgrown by ivy and brambles allude to death. Similar symbolism occurs in certain books by Blake, for example, *The Book of Thel*, 1789, copies of which were owned by George Cumberland, also a member of Bristol's sketching society.

Samuel and Richard Redgrave wrote of Danby with reference to this picture 'He sought to treat his painting as a poem, and to give ideal interest to his works'. The Romantic poets – Shelley, Keats, Coleridge – had seen nature as an almost godlike being, aware of human feelings. Hence the concept of the 'pathetic fallacy' – that landscapes and trees reflect human emotions. Here, the gloomy trees and sinister plants mirror the girl's mood of desolation, even death.

This poetic mood is linked to a realistic approach – a piquant combination unusual in the artist's later works. The figure is not sentimentalized; indeed, Palmerston, reflecting Victorian taste, complained that she was ugly. Nature is realistically observed: notably the direct, almost naively treated plants and flowers, anticipating the Pre-Raphaelites in its detail. Other sketches from nature by Danby indicate that this spot on the River Frome actually existed.   S.P.

Richard Parkes Bonington 1802–1828
British School
CORSO SANT'ANASTASIA, VERONA
Water-colour, 23.5 × 15.8 cm
Signed *RPB.1826*
3047–1876. *William Smith Bequest.*

During a tragically brief career Bonington produced a large
oeuvre of historical pictures, highly regarded in their time,
as well as the many atmospheric landscapes in oil and water-
colour on which his reputation chiefly rests today. Bonington
was born in 1802, the year of the Peace of Amiens, during
which English topographical artists, including Turner and
Girtin, flocked to travel abroad seeking picturesque views in
war-ravaged Napoleonic Europe. Following the peace of 1815
Bonington accompanied his father, a landscape and portrait
painter, to France. There he became a pupil of Louis Francia in
Calais and later of Baron Gros in Paris. Of all English artists of
the period Bonington seems to have had the greatest sympathy
with, and in turn some influence upon French painters. French
interest in English landscape and water-colour painting was at
its height during the 'Anglomania' of the 1820s when Parisian
connoisseurs and painters 'discovered' Turner and Constable,
whilst Bonington under the influence of Delacroix's painterly
and romantic work took up oils in about 1824 and executed
lithographs for the celebrated illustrated book, *Voyages
Pittoresques.*

Bonington travelled widely, visiting Italy for the first time in
1822 and again in 1826, from which year dates this water-
colour of Verona. It shows the Corso Sant'Anastasia and the
Palace of Principe Maffei, and is a typical view of picturesque
old buildings surrounded by the bustling life of the populace
wearing colourful costumes much favoured by Bonington and
his fellow romantic topographers such as Thomas Shotter Boys
and Samuel Prout.   S.C.

Samuel Palmer 1805–1881
British School
IN A SHOREHAM GARDEN
Water-colour, 28.2 × 22.3 cm
P.32–1926. *Bought from A H Palmer (the artist's son)*

Samuel Palmer spent seven years in the idyllic Kent village of Shoreham, between 1826 and 1833. There he lived a cloistered life. In common with his close band of friends, known as the 'Ancients', Palmer abhorred the onslaught of industrialization and materialism that dominated the age. He sought solace from the harsh outer world in the beauty of nature, and longed for the return of the 'Golden Age of Merry England'. Shoreham provided him with a perfect sanctuary to develop his highly personalized vision.

Influenced heavily by the Bible, the poems of Milton and his mentor William Blake, who taught him to see 'the soul of beauty through the forms of matter', Palmer's intense spiritualism found expression in the Shoreham landscape. *In a Shoreham Garden* is his most famous work from this highly creative period. From 1828/9 he made a series of seventeen drawings, in which he analysed the meaning of nature. Palmer's art depended on his individual response to the natural world around him.

In a Shoreham Garden shows an apple tree in an old-fashioned walled garden, the tree is in blossom heralding spring. The rest of the plants present a riot of colour more akin to the tropics than to the pastoral greeness of the English countryside. Most interesting is that the work has a deliberately unsophisticated technique. The colour is built up by clotted masses, achieving an effect of low relief. This is not noticeable in the apple blossom of the tree. Palmer's son noted that the apple tree in blossom 'curiously forestalls certain phases of modern art'. Palmer's style of water-colour work at this time was certainly contrary to the more fashionable broader washes and naturalistic tones used by established artists of the day, like de Wint.

Beyond the famous apple tree is a woman in a flowing red robe. Since each part of his work is imbued with symbolism, she has been called an 'Eve' figure, especially when one notices the creeper which looks like a serpent entwined round the trunk of the tree. Probably she is just the essential human presence in the landscape. So many of Palmer's landscapes were related to man, who provided a scale and order amidst nature's exuberant fecundity.

A.N.

J M W Turner 1775–1851
British School
LIFE-BOAT AND MANBY APPARATUS GOING OFF TO A
STRANDED VESSEL MAKING SIGNAL (BLUE LIGHTS) OF
DISTRESS
Oil on canvas, 91.4 × 122 cm
FA.211. *Sheepshanks Gift.*

Turner, as an artist, was enthralled by storms at sea, which he
painted on many occasions. This powerful painting comes from
the middle period of his career, and shows his ability to
capture the popular imagination with a work which illustrates
man's continuing battle with the wilder elements of nature.

The Manby apparatus was called after its inventor George
William Manby (1765–1854). It was a means of saving people
from a wreck by firing a stone at the end of a rope from a
mortar on shore to provide a lifeline to the ship in trouble and
was developed by Manby after he had witnessed a disastrous
shipwreck in 1807, when he was a barrack master at Great
Yarmouth in Norfolk. He was elected a Fellow of the Royal
Society in 1831, the year in which this picture was exhibited.

Manby's fame, and the dramatic and appropriate subject which
a depiction of the apparatus in use provided, probably
prompted Turner to paint this picture, but it is interesting to
note that John Constable also exhibited a painting of *Yarmouth
Pier* in 1831. Turner may well have got to hear of Constable's
plans, and decided to exhibit this picture by way of com-
petition. It seems very probable in any event that Yarmouth
Beach is indeed the setting he had in mind. He had visited the
town in 1824, and a water-colour exists in the British Museum
which depicts the firing of rockets on the coast there.

The painting may have been painted as a commission for the
architect John Nash (1752–1835), a friend of Turner,
or perhaps it was bought by Nash at the Academy in 1831.
He did not own it for long, for he died in 1835 and his
collection was then sold. At the sale, it was entitled *Blue Lights
off Yarmouth* and bought by John Sheepshanks, who gave it to
the Museum with the rest of his collection in 1857.   L.L.

Eugene Delacroix 1798–1863
French School
THE SHIPWRECK OF DON JUAN
Sketch, oil on canvas, 81.3 × 99.7 cm
CAI.64. *Ionides Bequest*.

Delacroix's painting illustrates a dramatic moment in Byron's poem, *Don Juan*, when the survivors of the shipwreck are casting lots to decide who it should be who will be sacrificed to feed his starving companions (Canto II, Stanza 75) adrift on the sea

> 'The lots were made, and mark'd, and mix'd, and handed
> In silent horror.'

Delacroix has been hailed as the leading light of 'Romantic' painting and he frequently drew upon the works of Byron, Dante, Goethe and Shakespeare for his subjects. His claim to this distinction lies in the fact that he did not attempt to develop a Romantic style but, instead, found a style which was compatible with the Romantic attitude; which could be said to have its roots in Baroque Realism while displaying a clear rejection of the style seen in the previous generation's classical painting.

The Ionides work, which is not dated, is generally accepted as being a sketch for the 1840–1 painting of the same subject in the Louvre. In the Paris painting, however, the subject has been treated differently with fewer people in the boat. Owing to the date of the Louvre work, this sketch has, in the past, been ascribed a dating of around the late 1830s to 1840s. However, an earlier dating of the late 1820s has more recently been proposed for this unsigned work, based on comparative studies with other known late 1820s works, and on Delacroix's preoccupation with Byronic subjects at this period.

Shipwreck, emphasizing man's helplessness in the face of elemental nature, was a most popular subject in Romantic painting. Gericault's *Raft of the Medusa* (1819) is perhaps the most famous example, but Delacroix may well have been influenced also by George Cruickshank's engraving of 1825 and by Rowlandson's *Distress* which was engraved and which contains the figure of a man with his elbows on the gunwhale. Delacroix himself painted several related compositions and, in turn, influenced later artists' treatment of the subject.   B.B.

Sir Edwin Landseer RA 1802–1873
British School
THE STONEBREAKER AND HIS DAUGHTER
Oil on panel, 45 × 58 cm
508–1882. *Jones Bequest.*

Although it was painting dogs which brought his fame,
Landseer also produced other paintings with more human
subject matter, like this early work of 1830. The theme was a
topical one, for since the late 18th century the road system of
Great Britain has been transformed by the work of Telford and
Macadam, improvements accomplished not with sophisticated
modern earth-moving techniques, but by the back breaking
labour of stonebreakers and navvies.

Landseer skilfully contrasts the physical exhaustion of the
stonebreaker, seated with his ram's horn of snuff beside him
and his rough haired terrier for company, with his pretty
daughter who has brought him his lunch in a basket. In the
distance the smoking chimneys of the crofter's cottage hint at
the romantic belief in happy domesticity in rural poverty,
extolled by Robert Burns in such lines as

> '*The honest man, though e'er so poor,*
> *Is King o'men for a'that.*'

The subject of stonebreaking – manual labour at its most
exhausting – was used later by the Pre-Raphaelite painters
John Brett and Henry Wallis, and most notably in France by
the romantic realist Gustave Courbet in a controversial work
of 1851. Landseer's painting, with its emphatic sentiment,
belongs firmly to the older genre tradition, though it might be
described as a proto-realist work. As always, the sheer quality
of his handling of paint gives much visual pleasure, both in the
brilliantly observed still-life painting and the depiction of the
stonebreaker himself, which anticipates the portrait studies of
Highland ghillies he later painted for Queen Victoria.   L.L.

124

William Collins RA 1788–1847
British School
RUSTIC CIVILITY
Signed *W Collins 1833* on the gate
Oil on panel, 45.7 × 61 cm
FA.27. *Sheepshanks Gift*

William Collins, born in London, the son of a picture dealer was described by a contemporary critic Richard Redgrave as a subject painter who occasionally painted portraits, but chose rustic groups and landscapes as his favourite form of expression. His art, says Redgrave was 'feeble, wanting in vigour and power,' but he added, 'through his happy choice of subjects his pictures will always be popular'. This painting is a half-size version, dated 1833, commissioned by John Sheepshanks, of the original, which was sold at the Royal Academy Exhibition of 1832 to the Duke of Devonshire for 250 guineas.

The subject matter illustrates an age-old state of society, by no means obsolete during the first half of the 19th century, when ragged, shoeless children of the poor could earn a copper by performing small services, such as holding a horse's reins, or in this case, opening a gate for a lady or gentleman to pass through. The oldest child of the little group touches his forehead as a sign of subservient respect for the mounted 'gentleman', whose shadow falls across the path in the

foreground of the painting. The chief originality of the work lies in the way in which the approach of the unseen rider is depicted, adding another dimension on the viewer's side of the scene. An engraving after the subject contained in the Parisian *Album du Magazin Pittoresque*, 1862, recognizing this aspect, entitles the painting 'L'Ombre du Cavalier'.

The road leading up to Montague House, Frognal, Hampstead, known as Montague Grove has been suggested as the location of the country lane, but though Collins is known to have lived for a short while at Hampstead, where in 1829 he 'temporarily engaged a house near the Heath', no positive identification of the location has been found. *Rustic Civility* was the first of three paintings with similar groups of country children; *Rustic Hospitality* and *Happy as a King* were also shown at the Royal Academy, in 1834 and 1836 respectively. Though all three were popular and were engraved, *Happy as a King* was perhaps the most charming of them, for its composition appears in a nursery wallpaper, produced as late as 1862.   J.D.H.

Friedrich Gauermann 1807–1862
Austrian School
WILD BOARS AND WOLF
Signed lower right *F. Gauermann 1835*
FA.78. *Sheepshanks Gift.*

In a dark and threatening forest, a boar protects his family and
eyes with suspicion the intruding wolf. It is a very nordic
forest, a type well known in Austrian painting from the time of
Altdorfer and the 16th-century Danube school, here adapted to
the greater naturalism of 19th-century Romantic painting.
Romantic, also, are the humanized animals, typical of the
period and very similar in conception to Landseer's. It is not
surprising perhaps that Sheepshanks, friend and patron of
Landseer, should have selected Gauermann as the sole foreign
representative in his gift of contemporary masters.

Gauermann was paid the high price of 500 florins by
Sheepshanks for this picture and it is clearly a major work.
He was one of the most popular Austrian painters of the time,
much sought after both by the Austrian aristocracy and by
foreign patrons, among whom *Schipings*, as he called
Sheepshanks, was only one of many. Indeed, when the Prince
Consort visited the newly opened picture galleries at the
South Kensington Museum on 19 June 1857 he singled out
Gauermann's two animal paintings: 'In looking through the
South Gallery, he noticed two pictures by Gauermann.
He seemed to know him and his works. "He was", said the
Prince, "Court painter of animals and he also painted the late
Emperor of Austria and all his family . . ."' (F M Redgrave,
Richard Redgrave, a memoir, 1891, p.174). There is no record of
Gauermann ever painting the Austrian Emperor and one may
suspect that this was a royal joke. C.M.K.

Sir Edwin Landseer RA 1802–1873
British School
THE OLD SHEPHERD'S CHIEF MOURNER
Exhibited RA 1837
Oil on panel, 45.8 × 60.5 cm
FA.93. *Sheepshanks Gift.*

This is one of the most famous of Landseer's paintings – it established his fame – and a picture that has come to represent the quintessence of all we associate with the word Victorian. It was painted in 1837, the year the young Queen ascended to the throne, together with a less well known companion picture *The Shepherd's Grave*, showing the same dog continuing to grieve at his master's last resting place, just as the famous Edinburgh dog Greyfriars Bobby was to do in real life.

It is easy to enumerate the qualities in *The Old Shepherd's Chief Mourner* which so appealed to the contemporary Victorian public, who eagerly purchased engravings of the picture which became one of the best loved prints of the century. Every detail of the composition develops a different thread of the story, successfully combining the themes of rustic piety, honourable but obscure old age, the dignity of rural poverty, and above all the value of loyalty and fidelity, expressed in the dog's devotion to his master. Most contemporary critics analysed the painting in this way, notably John Ruskin in a

famous eulogy of the work in *Modern Painters* in 1843, in which he described it as 'one of the most perfect poems or pictures (I use the words as synonymous) which modern times have seen'. But it is more interesting to try to understand why the Victorians cared so much about dogs. England is, and remains a nation of animal lovers, and was the first country to establish a society for the prevention of cruelty to animals, in 1824. The dog, the animal closest to man, was central to this concern, and Landseer's works perfectly expressed it in pictorial terms.

He was to paint many more famous 'doggy' pictures in the years immediately after *The Old Shepherd's Chief Mourner*, notably *Dignity and Impudence* and *A Distinguished Member of the Humane Society*. Although their anthropomorphic qualities – the association of human attitudes with canine behaviour – have at times been severely criticized, they have never completely lost their appeal, and recent exhibitions have confirmed the outstanding ability of Landseer as an animal painter.   L.L.

William Mulready RA 1786–1863
British School
THE SONNET
Exhibited RA 1839
Oil on panel, 35 × 30 cm
FA.146. *Sheepshanks Gift.*

Mulready was born at Ennis in County Clare, but was brought
up in Soho in London, and attended the Royal Academy
schools. After unsuccessful attempts at painting works in the
grand manner, he at first turned to landscape, augmenting his
income by painting scenery for the theatre. Such drudgery
must have been a distasteful experience for an artist whose
work is always distinguished by its extreme perfection of
finish. He was a slow painter, producing only two or three
pictures a year, but gradually he began to gain a reputation for
his small scale works dealing with his central preoccupations as
an artist, youth and age, childhood, and young love, subject
matter which though dismissed by John Ruskin as 'entirely
uninteresting' was to gain him considerable contemporary
acclaim. His works were greatly admired by the young Pre-
Raphaelite artists whom he taught at the Royal Academy.
They were to be deeply influenced by his advocacy of the
technique of using a white ground over which rich colours
were very thinly applied producing a glowing effect.

This technique can be seen to particular advantage in *The
Sonnet*. This small panel with its sonorous, jewel-like colour,
is very thinly painted, allowing us to perceive the powerful
quality of the life drawing in the figures of the shy young poet
and the girl who reads his sonnet. Their clothes, the trunks of
the trees and the rocky foreground have a luminosity achieved
by the thinly applied opaque colour over the light initial
priming. Yet this brilliant technique is controlled and
unobtrusive, perfectly conveying the artist's simple yet
moving theme. L.L.

Charles Robert Leslie 1794–1859
British School
A GARDEN SCENE
Oil on canvas, 30 × 40 cm
FA.130. *Sheepshanks Gift.*

Charles Robert Leslie (1794–1859) is seen today as a
'Victorian' painter, but in fact his earliest works exhibited at
the Royal Academy from 1813 on considerably predate Queen
Victoria's accession to the throne in 1837. Of American
parentage, he spent his early years in Philadelphia; a
subscription raised by its citizens enabled him to study
painting in Europe. From 1811 he studied at the Royal
Academy School in London. At first he made several attempts
at history painting, encouraged by his American friends
Benjamin West and Washington Allston, but soon found his
artistic niche in the humorous treatment of literary or
historical themes – starting with the popular success of *Sir
Roger de Coverley going to Church* (Royal Academy, 1819).

A Garden Scene (1840) is unusual for Leslie in its contemporary
subject matter. The artist's youngest son, George Dunlop
Leslie, later to become an artist himself, is shown at play with
his horse and cart in the back garden of the artist's home off
the Edgware Road. In contrast to his exhibition pieces, Leslie
painted more personal works – portraits, young ladies,
mothers and children and even a few scenes of children – for
example *The Mother and Child* (1846) and *Children playing at Coach
and Horses* (1847). As is clear from his *Autobiographical*

Recollections (ed. Tom Taylor, 1860), he was very fond of his
wife and family, allowing them to stay in his studio while he
worked, and of childish fun and domesticity. In this, he was at
one with the Victorians who in their art and literature
revealed a preoccupation with childhood, with its innocence
and beauty. However, unlike many who worked in this vein,
he never became sentimental or moralizing.

The composition of *A Garden Scene* is simple and easy: the
curving boughs and the washing line interact, emphasizing the
child as the focus of this intimate scene. The colours – green,
red and white – are chalky, opaque and naturalistically
observed. Direct and indirect sunlight falling in patches over
the figure and garden creates a sense of the outdoors.
The influence of Constable, with whom Leslie became friends
and whose biography he wrote, is felt throughout this work:
in its en plein air setting, treatment of light and fresh
observation. In his choice of a domestic, tender scene the artist
may reflect his study of C17 Dutch genre painters such as de
Hooch and Maes. A certain theatricality in the use of light and
the child's gesture seems characteristic of Leslie, who loved the
stage.   S.P.

Charles Robert Leslie RA 1794–1859
British School
MY UNCLE TOBY AND THE WIDOW WADMAN from Lawrence
Sterne, TRISTRAM SHANDY, Book viii, Chapters 24, 25
Oil on canvas, 81 × 56 cm
FA.113. *Sheepshanks Gift.*

Lawrence Sterne's (1713–1768), comic masterpiece *Tristram
Shandy* was instantly successful when it was first published in
1760, and has ever since been acclaimed for its sardonic
portrayal of the comedy of human life.

The incident depicted in Sterne's novel shows the old soldier
Captain Shandy, normally happily occupied in re-enacting the
battle of Malplaquet in the peace of his back garden, under
siege from the amorous Widow Wadman: '"I am half
distracted, Captain Shandy", said Mrs Wadman, holding up
her cambric handkerchief to her left eye; as she approached
the door of my Uncle Toby's sentry-box. – "A mote, or sand,
or something, I know not what, has got into this eye of mine –
do look into it – it is not in the while". In saying which Mrs
Wadman edged herself close in beside my Uncle Toby . . .
"Do look into it," said she . . . "I protest, Madam" said my
Uncle Toby, "I can see nothing whatever in your eye."'

Leslie excelled at literary subjects of this type, much in vogue
in the early 19th century. This was his most famous composition, which he repeated several times, the first version of it
being shown at the Royal Academy in 1831. The light comic
actor John Bannister was the model for Uncle Toby.
The picture became for the Victorian public an instantly
recognisable symbol of flirtatiousness, and in the 1860s became
extremely well known as an advertising image. It was
reproduced as a polychrome transfer print on the lids of pots,
issued by F and R Pratt, containing Russian Bear's Grease
(gentlemen's hair dressing) and it is not too fanciful to imagine
a Victorian 'Widow Wadman' giving such a pot to her 'Uncle
Toby' during their courtship.   L.L.

Theodore Rousseau 1812—1867
French School
A TREE IN FONTAINEBLEAU FOREST
Inscribed on the back *Th. Rousseau vers 1840*
Oil on paper, laid down on canvas, 40.4 × 54.2 cm
CAI.54. *Ionides Bequest.*

Theodore Rousseau was a founder member of the Barbizon
school of painters, and a life-long friend of Jean François Millet,
the great painter of peasant life. They are buried side by side
in Fontainebleau forest. Rousseau's landscapes, unlike those of
Millet, are unpeopled, and at first sight can seem unremark-
able and prosaic. But closer study reveals their mysterious
power, and his remarkable ability to capture the sombre
beauty of the trees in the forest of Fontainebleau. Rousseau's
trees, more than those of any other artist, with the exception
of John Constable, are individual portraits rather than
generalized studies, as in this example, an oak tree which for
years bore the name of Le Rageur, a famous oak in the Chaos
d'Apremont.

A character in the powerful short story *The Man Whom the
Trees Loved* by Algernon Blackwood is an artist whose attitude
to trees closely resembles Rousseau's. 'He painted trees as by
some special divining instinct of their essential qualities.
He understood them. He knew why, in an oak forest,
for instance, each individual was utterly distinct from its
fellows, and why no two beeches in the whole world were alike
. . . he caught the individuality of a tree as some catch the
individuality of a horse . . . it was quite arresting, this way he
had of making a tree look almost like a being-alive.
It approaches the uncanny.'   L.L.

Daniel Maclise 1806–1870
British School
WATERFALL AT ST NIGHTON'S KIEVE, NEAR TINTAGEL
Signed *D. Maclise R.A. 1842*
Oil on canvas, 94.5 × 70.5 cm
F.22. *John Forster Bequest.*

This painting is, among other things, a souvenir of the friendship between three men; the artist Daniel Maclise, the novelist Charles Dickens and John Forster the biographer and man of letters. The three had become boon companions in the late 1830s and it was one of the happiest phases in Maclise's life before he fell prey to depression and hypochondria in later years. Maclise sketched the spot which forms the background to this painting, and from which it takes its title, when they were holidaying together in Cornwall in the autumn of 1842. The artist afterwards began a painting using Dickens' sister-in-law, Georgina Hogarth as a model. Dickens bought the painting through an intermediary, believing perhaps that if he declared his desire to own it, Maclise would either give it to him or suggest a ridiculously low price. The revelation of this subterfuge was much to Maclise's chagrin. John Forster purchased the painting from the sale of Dickens' effects after his death and bequeathed it to the Victoria and Albert Museum as part of the Forster collection, which is notable for containing the manuscripts of many of the most celebrated Dickens novels.

St. Nighton's Kieve is a beauty spot in Cornwall which has attracted visitors, since the beginning of the 19th century. Along a gorge, the river has worn away many caves and potholes including the basin into which a waterfall plunges. The water then escapes through a hole in the side of the basin and tumbles over some rocks. It is this basin that has been given the name kieve, a Cornish word for bowl or cauldron. The origin of the first part of the name is more obscure and in the last century it varied between Nathan, St. Nathan, Knighton, Nectan and Neot.

The dark background, careful rendering of the plant life growing from the rock and of the bubbles in the stream, do not seem to be in the same world as the brilliantly lit figure of the girl, on whom all the colour in the painting is concentrated. As in many of Maclise's paintings there is something theatrical in the way that the figure has been posed against a backdrop.

Nevertheless, the combination of dramatic scenery, feminine beauty attired in peasant fancy dress, the domestic touch of carefully rolled stockings inside shoes on a nearby stone, and the serious expression of the dripping wet lapdog, give the painting its great appeal.   E.C.

Richard Redgrave 1804–1888
British School
THE GOVERNESS
Signed and dated *1844*
Oil on canvas, 91.5 × 71.5 cm
FA.168. *Sheepshanks Gift.*

Richard Redgrave played a pioneering role in English painting of the late 1840s. After leaving the Royal Academy Schools in 1826, he concentrated on historical genre pictures, but later painted some of the earliest contemporary subjects with a social purpose, called 'social teachings' by critics of the period.

The Governess was commissioned in 1844 by the collector John Sheepshanks as a version of *The Poor Teacher* exhibited at the Royal Academy in 1843. This original painting had been very successful: it was hung 'on the line' – that is, in a position clearly visible to spectators – which was an honour for an RA Associate such as Redgrave. In all, the artist painted four versions of it and its image was later engraved.

The Poor Teacher presents a pathetic scene: a beautiful, pale lady is seated alone in a schoolroom holding a black-edged letter, obviously downcast and presumably musing sadly about home and family, as suggested by the music on the music stand, 'Home, Sweet Home'. Sheepshanks had 'objected to the terrible loneliness of the forlorn governess in the empty schoolroom' (F M Redgrave, *Richard Redgrave, C.B., R.A., A Memoir*, 1891) and so the artist added to *The Governess* three pupils playing happily in a sunlit background.

One of the reasons why Redgrave changed the work's title to *The Governess* may have been to make the picture more topical and overtly propagandist. In 1843 a campaign had been started by the press to clarify and improve the ambiguous status of the governess, who acted both as servant and mistress, but was in fact neither. Jane Eyre in Charlotte Bronte's novel is a famous example in literature, but there are many other instances. Working as a governess was one of the few ways by which a single woman in the 19th century could earn a living.

Something more personal may also have prompted this theme: we know that Redgrave's 'beautiful, charming' sister Jane had caught typhoid while employed as a governess and died in 1829. Perhaps indeed, her early death may have been the stimulus behind his 'social teachings' since they deal exclusively with the theme of suffering womanhood. In a letter in the 1850 *Art Journal*, Redgrave himself wrote, 'many of my best efforts in art have aimed at calling attention to the trials and struggles of the poor and the oppressed'.   S.P.

143

Thomas Webster RA, 1800–1886
British School
THE VILLAGE CHOIR
Exhibited RA 1847
Oil on panel, 59 × 90 cm
FA.222. *Sheepshanks Gift.*

This painting has been on exhibition at the V&A almost from the day the Museum first opened its doors to the public. It is a much loved work and is splendidly documented.

It was painted for John Sheepshanks, the Leeds cloth manufacturer who gave his large collection of modern British paintings to the Museum in 1857. Webster's inspiration was a passage in Washington Irving's *The Sketch Book* (1820) which tells a delightful story about an old-time village choir. Thomas Webster was himself first destined for a musical career, and sang as a chorister at St George's Chapel, Windsor, before turning to painting. He became an RA in 1846 and belongs stylistically to the group of English genre painters who, like Sir David Wilkie before them, applied the methods of 17th-century Dutch painting to contemporary social scenes.

Webster found his scene in All Saints Church, Bow Brickhill, Buckinghamshire (although he altered the architecture to suit his composition) and drew his individual figures from the villages nearby. The painting was shown at the Royal Academy in 1847 and was described as follows in *The Examiner*:

'One hears the sound of each performer's voice; the growl of the basses and the ringing of the tenors; the conceited village clerk giving the time with an extended palm and clearly violating it with mouth agape, the spectacled and toothless admirer whispering in his ear, the waspish look of the violon-cello, who feels that his art has not had fair play, the hearty intonation of the fat farmer in the background, the emphatic feebleness of the smock-frock — all are excellent. The quaint prettiness of the little girls in front, too, with the boy friends in each other's grasp, and the tidy young couple singing off the same book behind, carry us out of the region of mere laughter into that of gentle character and homely English romance.'

When it was shown in the Universal Exhibition in Paris in 1855 the painting also found favour with Théophile Gautier and Maxime du Camp (associate of the great realist Flaubert). The painting belongs in the era following the Reform Act of 1832 and coincides with the great period of Dickens. (Webster exhibited *Dotheboys Hall* in 1848). Such choirs fell away as organs and harmoniums were installed in churches, a transition recorded by Thomas Hardy — recalling his childhood as a chorister in the 1840s — in *Under the Greenwood Tree* (1872). As was said of Webster in *Men of the Time* (1856): 'By and by his works will be historical, in addition to their other merits'.

M.H.B.

Jean-François Millet 1814–1875
French School
THE WOOD SAWYERS
Oil on canvas, 57 × 81 cm
CAI.47. *Ionides Bequest.*

Millet was born into a Norman peasant family. His emigration to Paris was as typical of his kind as his subsequent feelings of isolation. His experiments with different styles illustrate his search to convey experience which was at once personal and universal. *The Wood Sawyers* cannot date from much earlier or much later than his move to Barbizon in 1849, the village on the edge of the forest of Fontainebleau which was to become the focal point of a landscape group. Even before then he had been inspired by the activities of the Paris *banlieu*, the semi-rural, semi-urban life of peasant migrants with whom he could so closely identify. At the same time he began to base his drawings on the direct observation of unposed models. A study for this picture illustrates Millet's efforts to make his image of the man's violent action really convincing, to find a creative parallel to the real world.

The Wood Sawyers is an energetic presentation of physical labour, using strong contrasts of light and shade to dramatize the exertion. Detail is sacrificed to the overall silhouette. *The Athenaeum* in 1896 remarked that 'the exaggerated disproportions of the figures are such as actually to assist in intensifying the expressiveness of their attitudes'. Millet himself declared 'They say that one does see handsome peasants . . . but their beauty resides not in their faces . . . it emanates from the total effect of a figure and its actions . . . Beauty is expression'. His use of colour is daring, as we see in the intense blue of the breeches of the nearer sawyer.

That feature, and the picture's sustained force of rhythm, links Millet with his contemporary Daumier, to whom it was once ascribed. Both artists manage to combine immediacy with mythic power. Whilst the left-hand sawyer is compressed to convey the effect of drawing the saw through the log, the weight of the right-hand figures is balanced on a pyramid of his solidly braced legs; and his form, which echoes Michelangelo, links *The Wood Sawyers* with the emergence of an 'epic naturalism' in Millet's work of the 1850s, exemplified by the explosive, heroic, almost sacred figure of *The Sower*. Millet made his mission to depict the rhythms of the peasant's life in relation to the cycles and seasons of the earth: his achievement lies in the expression of the peasant's toilsome experience, of the interdependence and mutual expressiveness of Man and Nature.

M.R.K.

146

147

François Louis David Boçion 1828–1890
Swiss School
LUGGAGE BOAT ON LAKE GENEVA
Signed, centre on board, *1855 F. Bocion*
Oil on millboard, oval, 23.5 × 32.5 cm
1594–1869. *Townshend Bequest.*

Filmgoers with long memories will remember Orson Welles in
the *Third Man*, in the culmination of a speech advocating
violence, dismissing Swiss culture in a single sentence.
'And what did they produce?', he asks contemptuously:
'the cuckoo clock'.

Thanks to the bequest of the Rev. C H Townshend (d.1868)
the V&A has a large collection of 19th-century Swiss paintings
which should, by itself, give the lie to Welles' slanderous
remark. Townshend, a friend of Dickens and a passionate
collector not only of pictures and drawings but also of gem
stones and cameos, Swiss coins, glass, watches and geological
specimens, spent his winters in Lausanne and was personally
acquainted with the principal Swiss painters of the 1840s and
50s. One of his favourite artists was Bocion, by whom there are
sixteen pictures in the Museum. A native of Lausanne, he had
studied in Paris and returned home to recover from typhoid in
1849. His work, as typified in the painting, represents the very
fresh, naturalistic tendency which dominated Swiss art in the
mid-19th century. It may, in part, be ascribed to the influence

of Corot and the other French painters of the Barbizon school,
but it is worth remembering that Lake Geneva had provided a
focus for topographical painters from the late 18th century
and, indeed, Konrad Witz's *Miraculous draft of Fishes* (c. 1440;
Geneva Museum), a view of the lake painted 400 years earlier,
is usually singled out as the very first topographical landscape
in the history of European painting.

Bocion's many paintings of activities on and around Lake
Geneva are closer to life than those of his 18th-century
predecessors, but for his subject he was following in a strong
local tradition.

His technique was to paint broad, rapid sketches, of which this
is a typical example, in the open air and then to compose
larger, more finished pictures for exhibition, in his studio.
The *Luggage Boat* combines his lifelong interest in depicting
ships on Lake Geneva with his desire to portray people in
everyday attitudes at work or at leisure.   C.M.K.

Richard Burchett 1815–1875
British School
ISLE OF WIGHT
Oil on canvas, 34.3 × 57.1 cm
9108–1863

The *Isle of Wight* is one of those minor masterpieces by an
otherwise forgotten painter in which the history of Victorian
painting abounds. Burchett's activities as an educationalist and
art administrator are much better documented than his work
as a painter, even though he exhibited often at the Royal
Academy annual exhibitions from 1847. After studying at the
Birkbeck Institute, Burchett entered, in 1841, the Government
School of Design, then at Somerset House staying on to
become an Assistant Master. On the formation of the
Department of Practical Art in 1852 he was appointed Head
Master of the Normal School for Training Teachers.
In addition he found time to write and published two books on
Practical Geometry and *Linear Perspective*.

Burchett's career as painter and pedagogue is oddly paralleled
by that of William Bell Scott, another pillar of the Government
Schools, whose quirky genius was touched by the influence of
Rossetti and Ford Madox Brown. In Burchett's *Isle of Wight* it
is tempting to identify elements such as the use of clear bright
colour and the beautifully observed detail as Pre-Raphaelite.
Certainly it would seem that Burchett had seen and understood Ford Madox Brown's experiments in informal landscape
of the late 1840s, but perhaps the most important influence on
Burchett's style is to be found in the still under-rated
landscapes painted by that great luminary of the Schools,
Richard Redgrave.

Sadly almost no other canvases by Burchett are known to
survive. He died in Dublin in 1875 and was commemorated by
a tablet erected in the School of Art at South Kensington.   S.C.

John Frederick Herring, Senior 1795–1865
British School
SEED TIME
Signed and dated *1854–6*
Oil on canvas, 106.2 × 183 cm
P.19–1915. *Given by Miss Mercy Mayhew in memory of the late
Captain Alfred H. Mayhew.*

The works of J F Herring follow in the genre of British animal painting already established by artists such as Francis Barlow, George Stubbs, Ben Marshall and James Ward, a genre which responded to a native enthusiasm for sporting life and country pursuits, and to its patrons' demand for clear, accurate portrayals of memorable animals and events in the sporting and farming calendar. Herring took up painting in 1815, after an early career as a coach painter and later coach driver, and, despite little formal training, won speedy success with his naturalistic and polished portraits of celebrated racehorses. He also made a name for himself in the depiction of coaching, hunting and farmyard scenes, one critic complaining that 'Herring grows more and more of an agriculturalist', as he devoted increasing attention to rural subjects.

Seed Time shows ploughing and sowing in the Weald of Kent, and it is a finely balanced composition in which men, horses and machinery progress across the landscape in a stately sequence. The single file of four horses drawing the wooden plough, with their driver and the ploughman, lead the eye gently leftwards down the valley and to the coast beyond. That movement is reinforced by the four-horse team of Shires

pulling the weighted roller that follows after the plough, breaking up the clods of newly turned earth. A counter movement is set up by the besmocked figure at the head of the Shires, who, in turning to face his team, leads the spectator's eye to the sower broadcasting his seed. Behind the sower hovers a flight of eager crows, and they, together with a further team of horses in the middle distance, give the painting its balancing pull to the right.

There is no doubt that for all its naturalism the painting has a picturesque quality that makes no concessions to the rigours and hardships involved in working the land. The artful foreground grouping of the two dogs, with the walking stick, food basket, drinking bottle and coats, not only echoes the undulating shapes of the landscape, but also provides a reassuring note of domesticity. Kindly sunshine bathes the scene, illuminating the Weald in sparkling detail, highlighting the procession of plough and roller, and burnishing the horses' coats. With expressive, yet meticulous brushwork, Herring conveys a rosy picture of rural England that must even then have provided a pleasant antidote to the prospect of encroaching industrialism.   M.W.T.

152

David Cox 1783–1859
British School
THE CHALLENGE
Water-colour, 45.5 × 66.6 cm
1427–1869. *Townshend Bequest.*

The Challenge is not Cox's original title for this work. It is probably the painting exhibited in 1856 at the Society of Painters in Water-colours as *On the Moors near Bettws-y-Coed*. Cox visited the Welsh village of Bettws-y-Coed annually from 1844, probably because the open spaces of the Welsh hills and moors provided him with the right subject matter for the particular style of painting that he had developed. Throughout his long working career he was a consistent exponent of the principles of water-colour painting that had guided landscape painters in his youth: that landscape water-colours could provoke a strong emotional response in the spectator, especially if the natural associations of the subject were enhanced by the manipulation of the medium to suggest effects of atmosphere and space.

The Challenge is one of his last and most powerful works and represents his technique at its most extreme. He was particularly famous for representing the wind and the rain by means of short dashing brush-strokes laid on to one another on coarse rough-textured paper. By this means the turbulence of

the elements was suggested by the roughness of the paint surface. In *The Challenge* the downpour of rain is clearly suggested by the broad diagonal brush-strokes with which the whole picture is painted. The Welsh hills are relegated to a distant position in the landscape and the only inhabitant in this desolate landscape is a solitary bull, a symbol of animal power at its crudest and most basic. The whole picture is an almost impressionistic rendering of nature at her roughest and wildest, in both atmospheric and animal form.

The bull thus takes the place of any human inhabitant in the scene and faces the force of the elements by himself. In this respect *The Challenge* is a more evocative title than the original topographical one. The colours are dark and sombre and suggestive of approaching night and an oncoming storm. The atmosphere as a whole is threatening and full of menace and foreboding. We can feel the bull's discomfort in the scene and share with him his apprehension of what the night will bring.
                                                                    K.H.J.C.

154

John Frederick Lewis 1805–1876
British School
LIFE IN THE HAREM, CAIRO
Signed with the artist's monogram lower right *JFL 1858*
Water-colour, 60.6 × 47.7 cm
679–1893

At the end of the Napoleonic wars, the Englishman's long-repressed curiosity about foreign parts led to an ever-widening circle of foreign places recorded by our water-colourists and in their resulting publications. The movement, which had begun by surveying the medieval towns and ancient monuments of France and Germany, was increasingly drawn to warmer climes and more exotic cultures. By the end of the 1840s three artists in particular – Sir David Wilkie, David Roberts and John Frederick Lewis – had gone to Spain to investigate the people and the remains of the moorish-culture there and actually crossed the Mediterranean to study the life and the landscape of the Arabs of North Africa and Palestine. In this respect the English water-colour movement became less insular and partook of the general European interest in the culture of the Arabs; one thinks of the desert scenes of Horace Vernet, or Delacroix's famous trip to Morocco and Algiers in 1832.

Life in the Harem is both a record of this interest, and of one man's insatiable wanderlust. John Frederick Lewis, son of a successful engraver, was already a successful water-colour painter and society man when in 1837 he set off on a journey through Europe and the East that was to culminate in a ten-year-stay in Cairo in the years 1841–51. Here he spent his time in making endless studies of the people and life of the culture in which he lived, and on his return to London in 1851 he commenced a succession of scenes from Arab life in water-colours and oils that were to entrance the Victorians by their brilliance of colour and minuteness of descriptive detail. In style he cannot be said to belong to any particular artistic movement such as Pre-Raphaelitism, though he shared their concern for minute detail; he seems to have acted mainly as a kind of documentary reporter, telling the Victorian public about a culture that was still alien and foreign to them.

Life in the Harem is reminiscent of his first great success, 'The Harem' of 1850, but has a less obvious erotic appeal (that picture showed a new recruit to the Harem being exposed to her pasha). His mood here is infinitely more relaxed and she seems to be enjoying a quiet afternoon out of the sun while her maidservant brings her some refreshment. Note how Lewis brilliantly suggests the heat of the afternoon by his use of Chinese white to heighten the colours, as well as the depiction of the reflected light on the face of her maid-servant entering through the door. Yet we can sense that, for all her life of luxury, the girl is entrapped – not merely by the weightiness of her clothes, or the grid-like pattern of the verticals and horizontals of the room (a device that Lewis borrowed, like the mirror, from Dutch painting), but purely by the absence of any reference in the picture to any kind of life outside the Harem. Her one view through the window is that of a mosque, a symbol of the culture that left women few alternatives to the Harem. In many ways her situation is not dissimilar from that of an ordinary English upper-class lady of the 19th century – a cosseted doll kept on sufferance in a man's world – and it may well be that Lewis's appeal to the Victorians rested not simply on his superficial depiction of an alien and exotic culture, but also on his underlying implication that the basic assumptions about the organization of human society were the same throughout the world, East and West.

K.H.J.C.

William Powell Frith RA 1819–1909
British School
CHARLES DICKENS (1812–1870)
Signed *W P Frith fecit 1859*
Oil on canvas, 67.9 × 55 cm
F7. *Forster Bequest.*

John Forster, journalist, author and intimate friend of Dickens, first met Frith to discuss this commission in 1854. Frith's early paintings had depicted historical and literary subjects, but he found himself 'drawn to the illustration of modern life', and achieved his reputation with *Ramsgate Sands* (1844), purchased by Queen Victoria herself. A Royal Academician (1852), he exhibited internationally, but is best known for his panoramic genre scenes, *Derby Day* (1858) and *The Railway Station* (1862). Frith's canvases epitomize the spirit of the age as meaningfully as the characters of Dickens' novels.

'Dickens,' wrote Frith, 'had reached the topmost rung of a very high ladder,' as an author and campaigner for social reform. Forster was unimpressed when Dickens began to grow a moustache, and instructed Frith to 'wait until the hideous disfigurement is removed,' before beginning the portrait. Four years later, appalled to discover that Dickens had grown a beard, Forster ordered Frith to begin work immediately, lest whiskers follow, obscuring even more of Dickens' face.

To assist the artist, Mr Watkins photographed Dickens, but Frith found the images unhelpful. Dickens 'sat delightfully,' and was 'most pleasant. No wonder people like him.' Frith discarded the conventional column and curtain setting, and depicted the author at work in his study at Tavistock House. Dickens is writing *A Tale of Two Cities*, and *David Copperfield* and another bound volume lie nearby. Behind him a calendar and an address from the City of Birmingham are displayed.

Frith records that Dickens arrived at the studio 'wearing a large, sky-blue overcoat. I protested that I could not manage the overcoat.' Dickens sits, elegant in black. 'What a face to meet in a drawing room!' wrote Leigh Hunt, 'It has the life and soul . . . of fifty human beings.' The bright, enquiring eyes and powerful forehead are enhanced by the shadowy background.

Forster paid Frith 300 guineas for his pains and was delighted with the portrait. He bequeathed this picture and many other paintings and manuscripts to the Museum.   A.B.

Myles Birket Foster RWS 1825–1899
British School
THE MILKMAID
Signed and dated *BF 1860*
Water-colour, 29.7 × 44.5 cm
520–1882. *John Jones Bequest.*

The theme of the milkmaid as a symbol of vulnerable
innocence and youthful beauty has a long history in English art
and literature. It can be found in Shakespeare's plays, George
Morland's paintings, the bawdyness of 18th-century ballads,
and the tragic inevitability of the fate of Thomas Hardy's
heroine Tess of the D'Urbervilles. Birket Foster's milkmaid,
his most famous composition, serene in her rustic vigour and
comeliness, occupies an important place in this tradition,
and served for the Victorian urban public as a potent and
nostalgic visual reminder of their rural roots.

Birket Foster's immense contemporary popularity as a water-
colour painter is one of the most interesting aspects of
Victorian art. He enjoyed the somewhat dubious distinction of
being one of the most extensively copied of all Victorian
artists. His works were duplicated with loving enthusiasm by
generations of emulative artists who sought to capture the
secret of his infallible formula of pretty girls or children and
domestic animals portrayed in peaceful landscapes reminiscent
of Constable's paintings. Inevitably over the years, many of
these copies have gained fraudulent signatures, and are now
passed off as genuine works. But where they fail, and where
Foster succeeded, was in the surprising power of his underlying life drawing, and the vigorous freedom of his landscape
sketches, concealed by his elaborately stippled water-colour
technique.   L.L.

Henri de Braekeleer 1840–1888
Belgian (Antwerp) School
A FLEMISH GARDEN: LA COUPEUSE DE CHOUX C.1864
Signed lower right Henri de Braekeleer
Oil on canvas 47.6 × 58.4 cm
CAI 88. *Ionides Bequest.*

Henri de Braekeleer was born in Antwerp and became the pupil of his uncle, the history painter Henry Leys, who took a special interest in him. As part of his training Leys took his nephew to churches and other ancient buildings, encouraging him to sketch precise architectural details, even sending him to Wittenburg to provide sketches of Martin Luther's house for one of Leys' own paintings. This journey kindled a life-long interest in the Reformer and Braekeleer became a devoted reader of the Bible. His early training in exact observation and rendering of detail stood Braekeleer in good stead, for he won a gold medal at the Brussels exhibition of 1872 and at the universal exhibition in Vienna the following year, becoming one of the best-known painters of the 19th-century Belgian School.

He is said to have much admired the work of Vermeer, but he did not slavishly copy him or his technique. Braekeleer was in the mainstream of Flemish painting however, and did share some of that artist's obsession with the portrayal of the fine details of the ordinary world, in buildings, costume and natural forms. The heightened sense of reality infuses Braekeleer's paintings of potentially mundane subjects with an indefinable atmosphere of melancholy, of something secret but almost tangible beyond surfaces and appearances in a way which looks back to Pieter de Hooch and foreshadows the work of Fernand Khnopff, especially in that artist's pictures of Bruges.

162

This precisely rendered scene of a vegetable garden in late summer is similar in style and subject to two paintings entitled 'Le Jardin du Fleuriste' which are in the Museums at Antwerp and Tournai. The theme of a woman in peasant costume cutting a humble cabbage seems ordinary enough when described in words but the lovingly painted details, such as the grey-green bloom on the leaves of the cabbages, the reassuring solidity of the ancient brickwork and the profusion of plants have an intensity which transcends the simplicity of the subject. The choice of view point is very subtle, reminiscent of Pieter de Hooch. The path to the alleyway intrigues the viewer, leads the eye to the courtyard glimpsed beyond and arouses curiosity about the other side of the buildings in the background.

Braekeleer painted other scenes in the manner of Flemish old masters, complete with historical trappings, but the common factor of all his paintings was the lack of violent movement, a desire for silence and contemplation, broken only by calm, deliberate useful actions; and a dislike for the commercial bustle of the modern world.   C.N.

Josephus Laurentius Dyckmans 1811–1888
Belgian (Antwerp) School
GRANDMOTHER'S BIRTHDAY (LA FÊTE DE LA GRAND'MÈRE)
Signed and dated lower left J L Dyckmans 1867
Oil on oak panel, 48.3 × 39.7 cm
I–1871. *Given by Frederick Heusch.*

J L Dyckmans was born at Lier in Holland and settled in Antwerp in 1833, where he joined the studio of Wappers. Dyckman's genre scenes became very popular; the Victorian public liking very much the photographic minuteness of detail and the smoothness of finish in his paintings. His reputation grew so much that he was known as the 'Belgian Dou', his admirers comparing his work to that of Rembrandt's pupil Gerrit Dou, who was said to have painted with the aid of the magnifying glass.

This painting was made during the artist's residence in London, presumably for Frederick Heusch, who bequeathed this picture to the Museum in 1871. The 'Grandmother' in the picture was Mrs Sarah Heusch, the donor's mother. It illustrates very well Dyckman's technique which was reputed to have had a 'porcelain smoothness'. The reason for this comparison is that the artist used a carefully prepared brilliant white ground (a technique also used by the Pre-Raphaelites), on which the colours were laid with extreme care in very thin glazes, with especial emphasis on the flesh tints. A luminous effect is thus obtained, similar to painting on a small scale on white translucent porcelain in vivid enamel colours, perfected first by the Chinese potters.

The same care that Dyckmans lavished on the facial details was put into the rest of the picture, into the knots of the carpet, the lace cap, collars and cuffs, the heavy watered silk of the adults' dresses and even the woven furnishing silk on the chairback. The vase of flowers is a miniature Dutch flower painting in its own right. The whole scene is a classic illustration of high Victorian interior design; more useful to historians than a photograph, it is in full accurate colour, reproducing exactly even the chemical dyes of the carpet.

Photography may have played a bigger part in this painting than hitherto suspected. If the information on an old label is correct, Mrs Sarah Heusch died in 1864. Her features and pose on this posthumous portrait of 1867 may have been painted from a Daguerreotype or photograph, whereas the mother and child were painted from life. Presumably Frederick Heusch wanted a family portrait which would include the image of his deceased mother and commissioned Dyckmans to compose one with artist's licence. This would explain the slightly awkward composition, the Grandmother rigidly relaxed in the pose adopted by sitters for Daguerreotypes in the 1850s, which the painter retained in this picture. Dyckmans may have been forced to resort to a lay-figure to achieve the lifelike draping of the dress, its folds and texture, which would account for the slightly hesitant mother and child not really looking at Grandmother. This picture therefore represents convergence of two forms of intense reality; the historic Netherlandish concern for the detailed portrayal of everyday life and the unselective recording of minute detail in photography.   C.N.

164

Honore Daumier 1808–1879
French School
THE PRINT COLLECTORS
Water-colour, 34.5 × 31.1 cm
CAI.118. *Ionides Bequest*.

Throughout his life as a busy caricaturist Daumier's chief
concern was the endless production of lithographs. He drew
over 4,000 during his career, hoping he said, that each one
would be the last. But in the years 1860 to 1864 he briefly
severed his lifelong association with the satirical magazine *Le
Charivari* and devoted himself to painting.

His subjects fell into two main categories. The first, pictures
drawn from everyday life, afforded an urban counterpoint to
Millet's peasants, in scenes implicit with social comment,
depicting railway carriages, waiting rooms, workers, lawyers
and criminals, and incidents in the Parisian streets.

The second category of subjects favoured by Daumier were
pictures of collectors and connoisseurs, looking over artist's
shoulders or pouring over portfolios of choice prints, as in this
picture. It has been said that Daumier chose such subjects
because they sold well, appealing to collectors who saw their
interests reflected as in a mirror held up to nature. But their
saleability alone cannot account for Daumier's fascination for
the subject, to which he returned so often. In the words of
Henry James' memorable essay on Daumier, in them we see
reflected 'the old Parisian quay, the belittered print-shop,
the pleasant afternoon, the glimpse of the great Louvre and
the other side of the Seine, . . . *estampes* suspended in the
window and doorway . . . extracted, piece by piece from musty
portfolios'. In such works Daumier captured the essence of the
whole disease of collecting, and it is appropriate that the
present example should have been owned by the great
collector Constantine Alexander Ionides, who gave it to the
Victoria and Albert Museum with other fine examples of
Daumier's work, including a notable 'Railway Waiting Room'.

L.L.

Sir John Everett Millais
British School
The Eve of St Agnes
Water-colour, 20.3 × 26 cm
D.141—1906. *Purchase from the collection of P H Rathbone.*

Millais is always remembered for his precocious talent for painting and technical ability. He exhibited a mammoth history painting at the Royal Academy at the age of 17 which paved the way for a successful career. The desire for success was the motivating force behind much of Millais' work, especially from the 1870s onwards when his style developed apace with sentimental but popular Victorian taste. However, the 1860s was a time of transition for Millais. In *the Eve of St Agnes* he harks back to earlier Pre-Raphaelite works, both in the choice and treatment of the subject matter.

Millais has depicted a scene from a poem by Keats in which the heroine performs an elaborate ritual in order to dream of her future husband. Millais has caught her at the moment when she is undressing, transfixed by the awe of this special night, the Eve of St Agnes. This water-colour is a version of the larger oil painting of the same subject exhibited at the Royal Academy in 1863, and now in the collection of the Queen Mother. Millais followed an exacting formula during the painting of the St Agnes, in keeping with the Pre-Raphaelite method of obtaining complete verisimilitude, as when he placed Lizzie Siddal in a bath of water to pose for his famous *Ophelia* of 1852. Millais journeyed to Knole Park and there in a freezing room, with the bed on which James I was said to have slept, he painted the oil version. For three nights Lady Millais posed in her bodice as Madeleine, the heroine of the poem, while moonbeams fell across her body at the required angle to produce the lattice shadow effect.

Millais was primarily a painter in oils, but his technical versatility enabled him to translate the ghostly mood of mystery of the St Agnes legend into the medium of water-colour. The study, probably painted later in the same year, shows an overall grey-green effect rendering the 'wintry moon' and atmosphere of Keats' poem. Even the blue of her dress enhances the coldness and trance-like quality expressed by Keats. Millais admirably captures the stillness and tension of the moment when the girl, transfixed, dares not look round for fear of breaking the spell.

Critics did not like the oil version when it was exhibited. Tom Taylor, a dramatist, referred to Lady Millais as that 'scraggy model' and Sir Francis Grant said 'I cannot bear that woman with the grid iron', referring to the shadows of the window falling on Lady Millais. Really the critics probably objected to Millais' return to Pre-Raphaelite methods, for as an evocation of Keatsian romanticism both the oil and the water-colour are perfectly expressed.   A.N.

Sir Edward Coley Burne-Jones, Bart., R.W.S. 1833–1898
British School
THE MILL, 1870–1882
Signed E B-J 1870 on the building on the right
Oil on canvas, 90.8 × 97.5 cm
CAI.8. *Ionides Bequest.*

This work was commissioned by Constantine Ionides in 1870, and in *Ion*, the history and reminiscences of the Ionides family, published by his son Alexander Constantine Ionides in 1927, it is indicated that the three dancing women are portraits of Marie Spartali (in profile to the right), Mary Zambaco and Aglaia Coronio, known as the Three Graces. Aglaia was Constantine's sister, Marie Spartali (Mrs W J Stillman), whom the artist considered the most beautiful of the Greek community surrounding the Ionides, and was also his 'model' for the painting 'Dance' (1870), and Mary Zambaco, the grand-daughter of Constantine, whose exotic looks and her misfortune caused Burne-Jones to fall in love with her. He embodied his distress caused by this attachment in the painting 'Phyllis and Demophoon' (1870), to which he gave the epigraph 'Dic mihi quod feci? Nisi non sapienter amavi' (Tell me, what have I done? Except that I have not loved wisely).

'The Mill' however, which he took twelve years to complete has that calm, dreamlike quality characteristic of many of the artist's works. The *Times'* critic commented when it was first exhibited at the Grosvenor Gallery in 1882, '. . . it reflects its

truth only from certain mental states'. Burne-Jones admitted that the painting made a deliberate reference, to be understood by 'the few people I care for' to his Italian masters, to the 'Primavera' and to the bathing figures in Piero's 'Baptism'. The mill pool, as *Ion* suggests, may be a recollection of the mill race at Alberga, or of the three mills near Oxford within a mile of each other at Milton, Steventon and Sutton Courtney.

David Cecil, comparing Burne-Jones and Samuel Palmer in his *Visionary and Dreamer*, London, 1969, writes that '"The Mill" lacks both the strangeness and immediacy of a vision. Rather it seems to depict a pensive daydream deliberately evoked . . . For his life is an illustration of . . . the predicament in which an imaginative painter found himself if he had the bad luck to be born in the 19th century'.

A wall tapestry after the painting, illustrated in the *Art Journal*, 1910, worked on linen in crewels by the Royal School of Art Needlework, omits the bathing figures in the background.

J.D.H.

Gustave Courbet 1818–1877
French School
L'IMMENSITÉ
Signed and dated lower left *69 G. Courbet*
Oil on canvas, 60 × 82.2 cm
CAI.59. *Ionides Bequest.*

Reviewing the recently (1901) bequested Ionides Collection in 1904, Sir Charles Holmes wrote of Courbet's paint surface as 'plaster or mortar or putty . . . but a short step from the spotty, lumpy surfaces of the Impressionists . . .' Such negative criticism may now be out of date, yet the same writer also spoke more admiringly of *L'Immensité*; 'When however, . . . he is face to face with the grand impassiveness of nature, his own impassiveness makes him unconsciously more sympathetic. No other painter has so powerfully impressed upon us the stolid menace and vast desolation of the sea . . .'

Courbet spent the late summer of 1869 at Etratat, on the Normandy coast, a village popular with painters since the early years of the century. In 1864 he had written to Victor Hugo, thinking he might be visiting the latter at his seaside house in Guernsey '. . . I love the solid ground, the orchestra of flocks that inhabit our mountains. The sea! the sea! with all its beauty it saddens me. In its joyous moods it reminds me of a laughing tiger, in its melancholy moods it suggests crocodile tears and in its howling fury a caged monster that cannot

devour me . . .' An ostensible preference for landscape but implying a strong attraction to the sea. In 1865 and 1866 he spent two summers at Trouville, where, as described by Gerstle Mack, he painted seascapes 'full of light and air, without a trace of social significance.' Three years later he made similar paintings, including the brilliantly clear-skied *Cliffs at Etratat after a storm*, in the Louvre and intensive studies of darker, angrier waters. Helene Toussaint observed that this was the first time he had used such large canvases with no animal or human figures. The Ionides painting, smaller than the large 'Waves' in the Louvre and Berlin is in type more daring: totally without human reference – not even a boat on the distant horizon. To quote Toussaint again, such treatment of water and clouds had been more part of the British tradition of painting although Turner and Constable 'had a strong influence in France, this aspect of their work was not readily understood . . .' Courbet's seascapes 'belong rather to the subsequent course of French painting than to its previous history.'   R.M.

Alphonse Legros RE 1837–1911
French School; worked in England
THE TINKER
signed; exhibited 1874
Oil on canvas, 115 × 132.5 cm
CAI.24. *Ionides Bequest.*

Alphonse Legros is chiefly remembered today as a Slade
Professor of Fine Art (1876–1894), whose teaching, together
with his predecessor's, Poynter, influenced some of the early
English Realist painters and the etchers Strang and Holroyd.

Born in Dijon, he studied about 1845 under the progressive
H Lecoq de Boisbaudran who emphasized training the visual
memory and allowed the artist to develop his individual bent.
Legros also copied Old Masters, such as Holbein and
Rembrandt, whom he admired throughout his career.
From 1857 he exhibited mainly religious pictures and modern
life subjects. Although critics, including Baudelaire, recognized
his early promise, the independent Legros found it hard to
make a living. With Whistler's encouragement and in the hope
of financial security, he moved to London in 1866 and began
teaching art.

The Tinker is a fine example of Legros' particular brand of
Realism. The Realist movement, from the 1840s on, was a
reaction against the earlier Neo-classical and Romantic styles.
Artists painted in a contemporary manner, recording the
world about them with sincere feeling. Mere literal representation was not enough, warned the Realist theorists: artists
should seek out the truth and evoke a picture's particular
emotion or mood to create a valid work of art.

Rural and peasant life, already threatened by the industrial
revolution, was favoured as subject matter. Traditional
craftsmen whose skills were passed on – tinkers, blacksmiths,
woodworkers – were depicted. Courbet saw the propagandist
value in such subjects, whereas Legros' concern with labourers
and peasants is that of an agnostic humanist, similar to
Millet's.

With sharp observation, bold draughtsmanship and solid
modelling, he portrays the itinerant tinker, absorbed in his
work and surrounded by his shiny pots and pans. His style
shows that he had learnt much from de Boisbaudran's teaching
methods, stressing the essential details and three-dimensional
effect of the figure. He emphasizes the tinker's presence by
placing him in the frontal plane, recalling Courbet's technique.
Legros in the 1860s had been among the first Realists to work
and place his subjects outdoors. The group of trees in the
background is characteristic of his style, as can be seen from
his numerous etchings of the French countryside. The bright
colour of the metal vessels offsets the other duller tones.
The *Times* wrote (1 May 1877), 'Here we have realism in its
naked strength'. Yet it is an ennobled realism: the man and
his work are dignified by the artist's evident affection and
respect for his subject, especially apparent in his treatment of
the lined face.   S.P.

174

175

Hilaire Germain Edgar Degas, 1834–1917
French School
THE BALLET SCENE FROM MEYERBEER'S OPERA 'ROBERT LE
DIABLE', 1876
Signed lower left *Degas*
Oil on canvas, 76.6 × 81.3 cm
CAI.19. *Ionides Bequest.*

Degas was fascinated by the stage, and by dancers, because of
the unusual lighting effects, and the exaggerated movements of
the performers. In a notebook of 1869 he wrote: 'Work hard on
effects of evening, lamps, candles, etc. The intriguing thing is
not to show the source, but the effect of light.' This scene is an
excellent example of his experiments since it combines three
separate light sources: the footlights, the gaslight in the flies to
simulate moonlight, and the desk lights in the orchestra pit.

Several aspects of the composition are strikingly novel for its
date: The low angle, as if *we* are part of the audience, and the
contrast of monumental style with a casual 'snap-shot' view.
(In fact, the seemingly arbitrary cropping and the sense of
spontaneity owe little to photography, which was still
academic rather than informal at this date, but are thought to
be derived rather from the asymmetry of the Japanese print).
This format, of a stage viewed from orchestra pit or stalls,
juxtaposing a dark and massive foreground with a hazy
brilliant backdrop, occurs several times in Degas' oeuvre.
For instance, there is another (upright) version of this scene,
painted in 1872, in the Metropolitan Museum, New York.

Meyerbeer's opera was first performed in 1831 and continued
to enjoy popular success until the end of the century. The plot

reflected a taste for macabre fantasy and 'Gothic' romance.
In this scene the phantoms of nuns, who had been unfaithful to
their vows in life, are conjured from the grave to entice the
hero Robert to ruin and damnation. There are five drawings in
the Museum, executed in the fluid oil-medium invented by
Degas and known as 'peinture à l'essence', of dancing nuns,
which relate, though not directly, to this and to the earlier
composition.

The picture also includes an informal group portrait. In the
foreground, which encompasses the orchestra pit and three
rows of stalls, are three identifiable figures, friends of Degas.
On the extreme left, looking out through his opera glasses,
is Albert Hecht, the collector who purchased the 1872 version
of the painting; next but one to the right, seen in full profile,
is Désiré Dihau, the bassoonist in the orchestra; the bearded
figure seen from behind towards the right is Vicomte Lepic,
an amateur painter.

In 1881 the picture was bought by the collector Constantine
Alexander Ionides. It was included in his bequest to the V&A
in 1900, and was thus the first painting by Degas to enter an
English museum. G.M.S.

Dante Gabriel Rossetti
British School
THE DAYDREAM, 1880
Signed lower right *D. Rossetti 1880*
Oil on canvas, 158.7 × 92.7 cm
CAI.3. *Ionides Bequest.*

The Daydream is one of the last major oils executed by Rossetti before his death. The idea for the painting was first mentioned by the artist in 1872, but hints of the composition can be seen in many of his earlier drawings of Jane Morris (the model for this work). There are also photographs of Jane Morris, posed by Rossetti in 1865, which show his preoccupation with a certain way of portraying his close friend and confidante. The mood of the sitter and the style of the dress that Jane Morris wears is particularly reminiscent of *The Daydream*. In fact this work perfectly expresses Rossetti's vision of women. For years he was obsessed by a particular type of female beauty, epitomized by his wife and model Elizabeth Siddal, and Jane Morris. The break from the Pre-Raphaelite Brotherhood in the early 1850s enabled him to develop a more personal poetic vision and explore themes from Dante and the idea of courtly love.

The Daydream is the culmination of his sense of fantasy and the way in which he wished to elevate and deify women he admired. A large woman seated in a highly decorative tree, with leaves resembling William Morris wallpaper, at first presents an odd juxtaposition, but as a portrayal of a mood the painting works very well. Originally Rossetti called it 'Vanna Primavera'. This is a reference to Dante's *Vita Nuova*, when Guido Cavalcanti's love Primavera is described as going before Beatrice as Spring precedes Summer.

From a lengthy correspondence with Jane Morris it appears that the painting presented Rossetti with many problems. The main one was to link the seasonal theme of Spring with appropriate flora, which would in turn enhance the overall design of the picture. The original drawing for *The Daydream*, now in the Ashmolean, shows Jane Morris holding a convulvulus flower. In the final painting honeysuckle was chosen, to match the rather full blown sycamore leaves of the tree.

The painting of the figure, especially the head and hands was reworked several times. There is a heaviness and lassitude about the female form which probably reflects Rossetti's own tiredness and approaching death. The static nature of the piece enhances the mood of dreamlike contemplation, summed up so well in a few lines from the sonnet Rossetti wrote to accompany the work:

> *'Within the branching shade of Reverie*
> *Dreams even may spring till autumn; yet none be*
> *Like Woman's budding daydream spirit fann'd.'*   A.N.

Gustave Moreau 1826–1898
French School
SAPPHO
Signed *Gustave Moreau*
Water-colour, sight size 18.4 × 12.4 cm
P.11–1934. *Given by Canon Gray, in memory of Andre Raffalovich.*

Sappho rests on a cliff top in an attitude of despair, seagulls and the setting sun symbols of death in the sky; the symbols of poetry are the lyre slung over her shoulders and behind her to the left, a pillar surmounted by the griffin of Apollo. From its subject matter the water-colour must be the first of the three episodes depicting the death of the Greek poetess; the other two are entitled 'Sappho flinging herself into the Sea' (in a private collection in Paris) and 'Sappho lying at the foot of the Cliff' (formerly in the Esnault-Pelterie Collection; the smaller version now in the museum at Saint-Lo).

Moreau exhibited a series of mythological subjects, including 'Oedipus and the Sphinx', 'Jason' and 'Orpheus' at the Paris Salons of 1864–6, but the style and complex technique of this water-colour, with its rich, jewel-like colours is characteristic of his later work.

A pencil drawing in the Museum's collection is inscribed *1 ere Danseuse Mlle Subra Opera de Sapho*, and though Moreau is not known to have designed for Gounod's opera of that title, it would seem that the subject was inspired by a visit to a revival of Gounod's work in 1884, and that all three paintings may be dated from about this year.

Certainly there is something rather 'stagey' about the composition, with the heroine seated in the centre in a semi-recumbent position in which an aria could be sung with comfort, a backcloth sky, and the pillar and part of the cliff as drop scenes. The same could be said for 'Sappho flinging herself into the Sea', for she falls in a graceful upright pose, holding up her lyre, as though supported on wires, instead of dropping headlong and sprawling into the sea.

Moreau's paintings were admired by Marcel Proust and by the Symbolists of the 1880s and 1890s, a group who reacted against the fin-de-siècle realism in art and helped to release it from a slavery to appearances. A key work of the Symbolists was J K Huysmans' novel *A Rebours*, which contains an enthusiastic description of Moreau's exhibits in the Salon of 1876.   J.D.H.

Ignace Henri Jean Théodore Fantin-Latour 1836–1904
French School
NASTURTIUMS
Oil on canvas, 62.8 × 42.5 cm
Signed and dated 1880
S.EX.24–1884

Simplicity of presentation and accuracy of observation combine
in this painting to produce something more akin to a
brilliantly coloured botanical illustration than the more
obviously composed flower paintings by which Fantin-Latour
is usually remembered. The artist has chosen not to show the
container the plants are growing in, and the plain background
makes the picture appear shallow in depth. The nasturtiums
fill almost the entire length and breadth of the canvas.

Fantin-Latour is perhaps best known for his flower paintings
but few resemble this one. Many of them show a vase of
assorted cut flowers set on a table, alongside other objects such
as fruit or tableware. These paintings of flowers found a ready
market in England and examples of these more conventional
bouquets are also in the collection of the Victoria and Albert
Museum.

Fantin-Latour lived in Paris but was able to sell most of his
flower paintings in England through an English couple, Mr and
Mrs Edwards, whom he had met in 1861. What began as a

friendship later became primarily a business arrangement.
Edwin Edwards would travel to Paris in the autumn and
purchase, from the artist's studio, works he thought he could
resell in Britain. After Edwards' death in 1879 his widow
assumed the role of Fantin-Latour's agent and propagandist in
Britain, and kept his work in the public eye by ensuring the
inclusion of his paintings in exhibitions all over the country.
The museum purchased *Nasturtiums* in 1882, two years after it
had been painted. It was acquired as a 'schools example' to be
sent round art schools in Britain for art students to study and
perhaps copy. A substantial part of Fantin-Latour's own
training had consisted of copying, mainly figure paintings,
in the Louvre in Paris.

Although a contemporary and associate of the leading
Impressionist painters Renoir and Monet, he did not share
with them their enthusiasm for the innovation of painting in
the open air. In all probability Fantin-Latour painted
Nasturtiums in his studio in Paris or at his cottage in
Normandy, where he and his wife spent their summer.   E.C.

Natalia Gontcharova 1881–1962
Russian School
Design for the backcloth of Scene II in *L'Oiseau de Feu*
Pen, water-colour and gold, 60.5 × 66.2 cm
E.2137–1932. *Given by Dr W A Propert.*

The Victoria and Albert Museum's collection of designs for the
Russian ballet is an impressive one, with fine examples of the
work of Leon Bakst, Alexandre Benois, Georges Braque and
Henri Matisse. To select one representative design is an
invidious task, but this example by Natalia Gontcharova,
the drop curtain for the ballet *The Fire Bird*, succeeds in
conveying the stylized brilliance which made the Diaghilev
ballets such a remarkable artistic phenomenon.

Like her husband Mikhail Larionov, Gontcharova was a
leading member of the Russian *avant-garde*, exhibiting with the
Blaue Reiter in 1912, and playing an important part in the
Rayonnist and Futurist movements. She first designed for
Diaghilev in 1911, and her work for the *Ballets Russes* success-
fully reconciled western trends with the traditional values of
Russian folk art and icon painting.

The Fire Bird (*L'Oiseau de Feu*) Stravinsky's first full-length
ballet with choreography by Fokine, was founded on a Russian
fairy tale and first produced by Diaghilev at the Paris Opera on
25 June 1910 with one set only by Golovin, and costumes by
Golovin and Bakst. This design was commissioned by
Diaghilev for the revival of the piece at the Lyceum Theatre,
London on 25 November 1926. The sheer power of the
glittering gold leaf, and the highly stylized treatment of the
onion-shaped domes combines to give the scene a dreamlike
quality suggesting unending vistas in a vast Russian city.

L.L.

Alexandra Exter 1882–1949
Russian School
STILL LIFE
Gouache, 33 × 25 cm
P.22–1976

Financial independence enabled Alexandra Exter to spend a part of each year in Paris, and in Italy, from 1908 to the outbreak of war in 1914. Already well-established in the artist-groups of Moscow, and her native Kiev, she was thus in an ideal position to inform Russian avant-garde artists about the revolutionary developments of Cubism and Futurism.

Cubism was a major influence on Exter's own work of this period. Picasso and Braque had evolved an intellectual analytical mode of representing the visual world: traditional rules of perspective and illusion were abandoned in favour of fragmented forms, depicting an object as it is known to be, rather than as it appears from a single view. One of the chief concerns of Cubism was to represent solidity and volume on a two-dimensional canvas without resorting to the obvious contradictions of an illusory three-dimensional picture space.

This decorative gouache of c.1914–15 shows how thoroughly Exter had assimilated these principles. The familiar Cubist motif of a musical instrument amid studio paraphernalia on a

table-top is presented here as a construction of flat angled planes. She has flattened the forms, but has nevertheless indicated volume and depth by making space a positive element in the composition. The hatched monochrome areas are symbols for the space between and around those coloured planes which make up the still life. The later phase of Cubism was directed by the invention of collage, as a fine art medium, in 1912. Exter herself used collage both in painting and design. This picture shows evidence of the influence of this technique in the simple abstract shapes, and the clear bright colour, which relates closely to certain works by Picasso of 1913–14.

On her return to Moscow in 1914 Exter applied her painter's training to the theatre, designing sets and costumes for the progressive director Tairov. Russian Modernism found its most complete expression in their dynamic integration of set and costume with actor and gesture. (A number of these advanced abstract designs are in the Department of Prints & Drawings). In 1923 Exter left Russia for Paris, and never returned.

G.M.S.

186

Percy Wyndham Lewis 1882–1957
British School
AT THE SEASIDE 1913
Pen and ink water-colour, 46.5 × 31.5 cm
E.3763–1919. *Gift of Captain Lionel Guy Baker.*

In 1909 Wyndham Lewis returned from nearly eight years of travel and study having visited major cultural centres in Spain, Germany and France. No works of Lewis' exist from this period and it is the years from 1909 up to the First World War that are considered a time of experiment and development of his mature Vorticist style.

Broadly speaking, Vorticism is an English hybrid of both the Futurist and Cubist movements. From Futurism it embraces the glorification of the machine age, the search for a universal dynamism through figures in motion and an aggressive iconoclasm against tradition aesthetics. From Cubism the Vorticists adopted the analysis of three-dimensional forms and their inter-relationship with the two-dimensional reality of the picture plane. Ultimately this led to the fracturing and faceting of the subject to present an almost abstract effect.

At the Seaside falls into this formative and eclectic pre-war period, showing a curious mixture of styles. The only obvious link between the subject matter and the title is in Lewis' use of colour. The subtle tones of blue, aquamarine and grey with touches of sandy yellow in the highlight areas of the machine figure (at lower left) enhance the nautical theme. The three

188

figures appear totally unconnected with each other although they are forced together in a loose pyramidal composition. The Futurist figure leads the eye across the picture plane in a strong rightward movement, while the background in bold strokes of blue and grey sweeps in the contrary direction. This represents one of the tensions within the water-colour. The bowler-hatted man is highly representational compared to his Futurist counterpart. He is attired in contemporary dress, but already there is a sculptural faceting to his form; his face can be read both straight on and as two profiles facing each other. It is as if he is poised on the threshold of metamorphosis. The rigid mask-like woman is dwarfed by these two more powerful figures and yet she recalls Picasso's studies with African masks. The lower part of her body has been overlaid with another piece of paper, producing a collage type effect and enhancing the experimental nature of the piece.

Lewis seems to be working out the case for both representation and abstraction at the same time in *At the Seaside*. Clive Bell, when reviewing Lewis's work in 1913 commented on this conflict. He said Lewis 'is inclined to modify his forms in the interest of drama and psychology to the detriment of pure design.'

A.N.

William Roberts 1895–1980
British School
SOLDIERS ERECTING CAMOUFLAGE AT ROCLINCOURT NEAR
ARRAS 1918
Pen, indian ink, water-colour and red crayon, 41.2 × 35 cm
P.94–1962

The artist described this drawing thus: 'The drawing was done toward the end of 1918. Its subject is based on the camouflage work I took part in, when the Arras attack was being prepared.' Roberts was sent to France with the Royal Field Artillery in 1916; in 1918 he was appointed Official War Artist, as were many of his peers, including Lewis and Nash. He completed two large oils as official commissions, but these were less effective works than the small informal drawings such as this. Although it has been squared up with red crayon, this was simply for decoration and no oil was worked up from the sketch.

Roberts displayed a precocious talent which won him a Scholarship to the Slade School of Art. In 1914, having travelled in France and Italy, he allied himself with the rebellious avant-garde of English art, the Vorticists. However, the principles of Vorticism, which combined the energy and dynamism of Futurist aesthetics with the fragmented form of Cubism, remained essentially a peripheral influence on his own fiercely independent style.

His first one-man show, at the Chenil Galleries in 1923, included a number of these war drawings. In the catalogue introduction Muirhead Bone praised them for 'a delightful quality of mordant irony'. The influential art critic

P G Konody, reviewing the exhibition, said: 'Mr Roberts proves triumphantly that his Weird Vorticist designs, with all their geometric distortion and grim caricaturist humour are based on powerful draughtsmanship and knowledge of form'. Konody exaggerates the influence of Vorticism on these drawings. Roberts had never been fully committed to the movement, and his allegiance was further weakened by the demands of realising actual observed experience. Vorticism was fundamentally an art of theory which failed to resolve the conflict between 'truth to life' and the radical use of pure abstract forms.

The anonymous figures owe little to Vorticism beyond a certain mechanistic style. Often in painting such formalization is an arbitrary device; here it is a purposeful and appropriate metaphor for the dehumanizing process of war in which men are stripped of their individuality to become machines of destruction. The angular forms also serve to characterize the devastated landscape. The composition has obvious icon-ographical parallels with the traditional representation of the Deposition of Christ – the camouflage blanket is a winding sheet, the blasted trees stand like crosses, whilst the actions of lifting and pushing could equally be interpreted as gestures of horror or supplication. It is an ironic comment on the terrible sacrifice of innocent lives.   G.M.S

Charles Ginner, CBE, ARA, RWS 1878–1952
British School
PORTRAIT OF BELFAST C.1928
Signed *C. Ginner*
Pen and ink and water-colour, 29.2 × 40.6 cm
Circ.420–1962

Ginner was born in France of British parents and was educated
in Cannes. He went to Paris to study architecture from 1899 to
1904 but abandoned that subject for painting, developing a
great admiration for the work of the post-impressionists and
especially for that of Van Gogh, Cézanne and Gauguin,
whom he regarded as the three major contemporary masters.
After a visit to Buenos Aires in 1909, where he succeeded in
selling some of his work, he settled in London late in 1909;
a date which proved to be of the greatest significance to the
development of his art. With his friends Gore, Gilman and
Sickert he formed the nucleus of the Camden Town Group,
which enjoyed its heydey from 1911 to 1913. With his close
associate Gilman he developed his theory of 'Neo-Realism' as a
reaction against slavish adherence to formulas derived from
Impressionism and a rejection of 'the slap-dash, careless,
and slick painting which has been and is still so much in
vogue'. He claimed in 1914 that 'The aim of Neo-Realism is
the plastic interpretation of Life through the intimate research
into Nature' and that 'This delicate research by the artist into
Nature, this collaboration, this objective transposition must
necessarily bring with it good and sound craftsmanship, a thing
sorely lacking in these days'.

After the death of Spencer Gore in 1914 and the even greater
loss sustained by Gilman's death in 1919 Ginner continued to
perfect his own personal, intense vision, pursuing his
preoccupation with form and pattern in the treatment of
subjects often conventionally unattractive. This major water-
colour drawing, probably dating from about 1928 (he was
painting Ulster landscapes in 1928, 1929 and 1930) superbly
demonstrates Ginner's mastery in water-colour of colour,
texture, light and atmosphere. The exactly observed
naturalistic details are wrought together in a mosaic-like
pattern which in no way detracts from but, rather, reinforces
the view of the industry and commerce of a great city
portrayed against the noble amplitude of its natural setting.

H.B.

Emil Nolde 1867–1956
German School
FRIESLAND FARM UNDER RED CLOUDS
Signed lower right *Nolde*
Water-colour, 35.5 × 47.5 cm
P.7–1964

Werner Haftmann, curator of the Nolde Museum in Seebull, writes tellingly of the roots of Nolde's art: 'It sprang directly from his native soil, that lonely, flat coast spread between sea and sky, up near the Danish border under whose tall sky, marked by flaming light effects and dramatic cloud formations, objects and people acquire a strange legendary quality. The setting itself strongly intensifies the visionary faculty of its inhabitants.'

Nolde was born Emil Hansen, adopting the name of his native village in 1901. As Haftmann points out 'It is as though he wanted, by taking this name, to mark his closeness to the earth.' He travelled widely: Denmark, France, Belgium, Holland, England, Italy; he taught in Switzerland from 1892–8; in 1913 the Imperial Colonial Office invited him to take part in an Expedition to the South Pacific. Yet he always returned to the Friesland landscape. From 1903–7 he spent many summers on the Baltic island of Alsen, with a studio on the beach, and from 1917–25 at Utenwarf, near Ruttebull, on the coast of Schleswig. When Utenwarf became Danish territory he moved back across the canal, to Germany,

to Seebull, close to the village of Nolde. At about the time this water-colour was painted, in the summer of 1930, while the house at Seebull was being repaired, he stayed on the island of Sylt in the North Sea, where he wrote 'I stared at the wild restless beauty of the evenings, when the last hovering clouds pass their fiery fingers across the vault of the sky and the light dies in smouldering, shifting colours.'

Northern Europe was more colourful to him than the South Seas. Travel enhanced rather than changed perceptions conceived virtually in childhood. Of his native landscape he had written 'I looked at the sky and the great clouds, they were my friends' but his experience, for example, of Chinese wash drawing may account for the simplicity with which he conveyed such thoughts in water-colours like this. Nolde was formally allied to the radical Expressionists *Die Brucke* in 1906 but his intense individuality made it difficult for him to sustain communal activity and although his work had and retained a powerfully expressionist character, he withdrew his membership of the group in 1907.   R.M.

194

Edward Burra 1905–1976
British School
SURREALIST COMPOSITION C.1934
Water-colour, 77.7 × 35.2 cm
P.6–1960

Edward Burra was an individualist and subscribed to no school or style, apart from his brief alliance with the English Surrealists (with whom he exhibited in 1936 and 1938), and his membership of the abstract art group *Unit One*, organized by Paul Nash, in 1933.

In a sense, though typical in colour and manner, this gouache is not representative of Burra's art as a whole. Most of his work was figurative, exaggerated caricatures in the style of George Grosz, with an emphasis on low-life and the exotic. His later work included still life and landscape subjects. His adoption of Surrealist principles – creating an alternative reality by the exploration of the sub-conscious mind and dream imagery in free association – was brief: from around 1929 (when he worked almost exclusively in collage) to 1934, at the latest. In his interest in, and use of these ideas he was in advance of his contemporaries, most of whom remained unaffected until the mid 1930's when Surrealist works were first exhibited in London. Burra had toured France with Nash in 1930, and they encountered Surrealist painting and collage in the galleries there, but Burra was already familiar with the work of Max Ernst, Magritte and others from German and Belgian magazines.

In this picture it is evident that he had absorbed much of the visual vocabulary of Surrealism, though this composition has none of the menace so characteristic of his low-life underworld scenes. The female figure who dominates the whole is a pastiche of elements from Ernst and Magritte in this period. The influence of De Chirico is apparent too, in the massive arcaded building on the right, with its long vista of blank windows, and in the heavy shadows. The small figure, left of centre casts a long shadow towards the viewer and this has been anthropomorphized by the addition of eyes, and of tiny claw-like hands and feet. Certain elements such as the white pseudo-Georgian folly to the left betray the English origin of the composition.

The perspective of the whole is illogical, and therefore disturbing. It is impossible to reconcile background and foreground, left and right. There are elements of 'trompe l'oeil' too: the emblematical rectangles above and below the arcaded building appear to have been stuck on to the picture.

In spite of the borrowings the style is distinctly Burra's own. The wit and vigour of his large water-colours (he never used oil) were much admired by fellow artists, and he was considered by Paul Nash and Wyndham Lewis to be one of the finest living painters.   G.M.S.

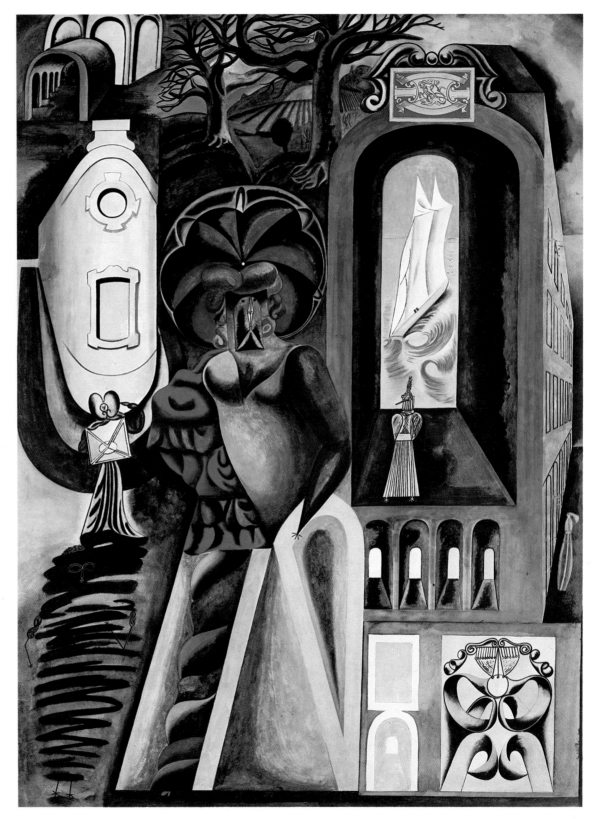

Ben Nicholson 1894–1982
British School
GOUACHE 1936
Gouache, 30.5 × 42.2 cm
P.2—1961

Ben Nicholson once said that he never thought of his paintings and reliefs as being essentially abstract. By this he meant that they were based on observation, and retained elements of representation. He had absorbed the basic tenet of Cubism, advanced by Picasso and Braque, that painting is an act of creation, not imitation.

This gouache of 1936 is one of a series of paintings, based on rectangular forms, done between 1935 and 1938.
The composition bears a superficial resemblance to Mondrian's grid paintings. Nicholson had visited Mondrian's studio in 1934: 'The paintings were entirely new to me and I did not understand them on this first visit (and indeed only partially understood them on my second visit a year later)'.
Thus Nicholson's debt to Mondrian was limited to visual and formal qualities. He adopted the primary colours combined with black and grey, but he worked with the rectangles in an intuitive way, quite unrelated to the intellectual systems of Mondrian. This picture and the related compositions are refinements of a remarkable still-life (*Painting – Trout*) of 1924, in which the subject matter was reduced to simple overlapping planes, treading a fine balance between the motif and pure abstraction.

The ideal of the work of art as a construction, a personal interpretation or recreation of the visible world, dominated Nicholson's art in the 1930s. It is apparent in this architectonic composition with its blocks of colour, vibrant primaries against soft blacks and dull greys. Though it does not derive from a rigid application of a goemetric system, the composition is remarkable for a pictorial system of unparalleled rigour and simplicity. This is all the more surprising since it was developed independently in a period when British art was generally insular and figurative. Nicholson himself was largely responsible for forging the links with the European avant garde which revitalized the arts in England in the 1930s.

In 1936–7 Nicholson was involved in editing *Circle*, an 'International Survey of Constructive Art', with sculptor Naum Gabo and architect Leslie Martin. His own commitment to Constructivism was embodied in his classic works, the white-painted reliefs, which he also developed at this time. These simple hand-carved literally 'constructed' pieces were prefigured in their proportions and in the disposition of the planes by the 1930s geometric abstracts.   G.M.S.

Paul Klee 1879–1940
Swiss School, worked in Germany
STIMME AUS DEM ÄTHER 1939: AN ALLEGORY OF
PROPAGANDA
Tempera and oil on brown wrapping paper, 50 × 38 cm
P.4–1965

The title is inscribed in the artist's hand – *Stimme aus dem
Äther*: '*und du wirst dich satt essen!*' (Voice from the ether:
'and you will eat your fill!'). Short hair, staring eyes and a
mouth dripping with saliva are the sitter's unpleasing
characteristics. The artist himself has provided the key to the
painting, for his personal catalogue entry in the Klee
foundation in Berne has the following addition to the title:
Kopf beim Anhören der Propaganda (Head listening to propaganda).
Klee, it appears, was portraying a German listening to the
propaganda of his leaders in 1939 with its promises of wealth,
plunder and *Lebensraum*. The quotation is adapted from
Leviticus 25.19: 'and ye shall eat your fill' and the head can be
interpreted as a portrayal primarily of greed whetted by
promise of Nazi propaganda, and also, to some extent perhaps,
of astonishment at the scope of these promises.

Thick, coarse outlines and features, a predominance of white
and an economy of line and colour may seem out of place
among the delicate intricacy, the charm and bright colouring of
most of Klee's work, but they are in fact typical of the output
of his last years. In 1933 he was dismissed by the Nazis, as a
practitioner of 'decadent art', from his professorship at the
Academy of Art in Dusseldorf, and in December of that year he
returned to his native Switzerland to settle in Berne. Within
two years of his return he began to suffer from the painful
illness of which he was to die in June 1940. From 1938 much of
his work contains the thick outlines and simple monumental
aspect discernible in this head. It is a style ideally suited to the
pessimism of his last years, dominated by his own illness,
by Hitler's triumphs and approaching war.   C.M.K.

Graham Sutherland 1903–1980
British School
THE WANDERER I 1940
Water-colour, 21.7 × 35.9 cm
P.20–1975

This sketch relates to Sutherland's first and only work for the theatre. He was commissioned to design two backcloths, and the costumes, for Frederick Ashton's ballet *The Wanderer*, which was first performed by the Sadler's Wells Ballet at the New Theatre, London, on 27 January 1941. The costumes attracted a good deal of criticism, but the two backcloths (the other was based on a painting, *Mountain Road With Boulders*, 1940) were much admired. They were considered to be most appropriate to Schubert's music and Ashton's choreography.

There is another version of this design in the collection of the Hon. Colette Clark. The two are broadly similar, but there are some variations of colour and detail. Both drawings have been squared for enlargement, but the process has been completed, by the addition of diagonals, only in the Clark sketch, which is in fact the one actually reproduced for the stage production. The V&A drawing is rather more detailed than the final version, which discarded the corn stooks, and the bushes to the left, and replaced the strong yellow with a glowing red. In its finished form the composition is more upright, and includes rather more foreground.

The strong, bright, rather acid colour is typical of Sutherland's work of this period, as is his method of using crayon with a semi-transparent wash, so that one colour shines through another. A low sun casting long shadows was a favourite motif, which he used to increase the dramatic character of the landscape. It also serves as a device to create a sense of space, which is otherwise lost in Sutherland's flattened forms.

Sutherland's inspiration at this time was drawn from the rugged scenery of the Pembrokeshire coast, which he had first discovered in 1934. He described the power of this Welsh landscape in 1942:

> *'The quality of light here is magical and transforming . . . Watching from the gloom as the sun's rays strike the further bank, one has the sensation of the after tranquillity of an explosion of light; or as if one had looked into the sun and turned suddenly away.'*

Light has the power to transfigure and metamorphose in these landscapes: they are imaginative 'paraphrase' rather than direct transcript. This brilliant fantasy landscape is very close in style and mood to the Pembrokeshire subjects, and it clearly reveals Sutherland's debt to the visionary works of Blake and Palmer.

G.M.S.

Paul Nash 1899–1946
British School
THE ECLIPSE OF THE SUNFLOWER 1945
Water-colour, 42 × 57.3 cm
P.19–1962. *Bequeathed by Mrs Margaret Nash, widow of the Artist.*

This water-colour, a version of an oil of the same title which belongs to the British Council, is one of a sequence of paintings in which the artist developed the symbolism of the sunflower and sun, based on the poem by William Blake which begins:

> '*Ah, Sunflower! weary of Time*
> *That countest the steps of the Sun*'.

The first of the series, painted in 1942 was entitled *Sunflower and Sun*. Nash wrote of this painting '. . . a shaft of sunlight breaking through the cloud falls across the form of a giant sunflower bowed by the wind . . . the drama of the event, which implies the mystical association of the sunflower and sun, is heightened by the two opposing eclipses . . .' He also compared the composition to that of *Pillar and Moon*, a painting completed in the same year, now in the Tate Gallery.

The Eclipse of the Sunflower and *Solstice of the Sunflower* followed in 1945, and a water-colour *The Sunflower Rises*, in 1946, but Nash did not live to paint the oil for which the last was a study, or to complete the final statement of his theme, which was to have been *The Sunflower Sets*.

The sun and moon symbolism, and the death of the gods during an eclipse is linked to the prehistoric ritual of the temples of Stonehenge and Avebury, and the presence of those giant megaliths in the Wiltshire landscape which fascinated the artist and inspired the dominant motifs of many of his works.

J.D.H.

204

Eduardo Paolozzi born 1924
British School
MASK WITH MOTOR CAR
Signed in blue biro and dated in ink lower right *Eduardo*
Paolozzi May 1958
Gouache and collage on paper (an unused shipping chart),
47.8 × 28.4 cm
P.31–1977

While Alice tumbled down the rabbit hole she fell to musing
on which latitude or longitude she might have reached, despite
the fact that she did not know the meaning of either word,
and how she might emerge: 'among people with their heads
downwards – the Antipathies, I think – '. In an interview with
Edward Roditi in 1959 Paolozzi despairs of the British ever
taking Surrealism seriously, unless it is apocolyptic and
religious as in William Blake or wonderfully nonsensical as in
Edward Lear or Lewis Carroll. If he too were a Carrollean type
he might be assured of serious discussion by English critics.

Alice's predicament on entering a strange world full of creative
opportunities and her doubts about the public world when she
re-enters it could be said to allegorize the position of the artist
and public reaction to him. Paolozzi has used a navigation
chart as a support in this work. Its demands for information on
situation (latitude and longitude), direction, speed and – just
on the edge of the sheet – destination, have been satisfied by
the image. It is as if the artist is saying: This is where I am,
this is where I am heading. Like Alice he might not be quite
sure where he will arrive, neither does he know what public
reaction will be, but the journey is necessary and positive.

206

'The intellectual prestige attached to abstract art in Britain' in
the 1950s was largely ignored by Paolozzi and his friends for
the sake of a more pressing need to establish the significance of
anonymous commercial and industrial draughtsmanship and
photography. (These interests were sanctioned by Surrealism
and Art Brut.) Paolozzi has picked a few examples of such
material and thrown them together. This suggests the random
way in which we apparently absorb the battery of images
which commerce and industry have brought to us. The shape
of the painted image, a head, further underlines the artist's
concern with mental assimilation. The work is without the
close cohesion of parts found in earlier 'Heads' of the 1950s,
neither does it have the directly Surrealist appearance of say
Psychological Sketchbook (1949) or the film *A History of Nothing*
(1960–2). The style of *Mask with motor car* appears to be
moving toward the more organized agglomeration of spatially
independent images which formed the basis of his early Pop
screen prints of the 1960s.   R.M.

Peter Blake born 1932
British School
TATTOOED LADY
Signed and dated lower right *Peter Blake 1958*
Black gouache and collage, mounted on red paper,
68.6 × 53.4 cm
P.3—1972

When Peter Blake gained a scholarship on leaving the Royal College of Art in 1956, he travelled Europe, pursuing his interest in folk art. In his tattooed ladies and pin-ups or night club dancers of the mid 1950s he deliberately reiterates the decorative style of fairground and circus where 'folk' art seems at its most accessible. Blake saw his work as a natural development of folk. i.e. in his own words he was constantly looking back at the sources of the idiom and trying to find the technical forms that will best recapture the authentic feel of folk pop. Tattooed ladies, interpreted as a technical form, offered a peculiar opportunity to an artist who was part of a movement where collage was essential to picture making. Here collage is no longer a chaotic aggregation of objet trouvé, as seen in Dadaist works of the 1920s, notably Schwitters, but an arrangement of separately spaced objects which can be read individually, like favourite postcards on a pin board. The collaged area is clearly limited, it is only part of, not the whole image: only the lady's body is tattooed.

A parallel interest: imitating collage and found objects, rather than using them, can be seen in Blake's now famous *On the Balcony* (1955–7) in the Tate. In the supports for paintings like *Loelia, World's most tattooed lady* (1955) he convincingly imitated the authentic panel on which fairground advertisments would be painted or posted. The V&A's Lady has facial features resembling 19th-century engraving or lithography, deliberately disparate (the eyes do not match) to suggest, without in fact being, collage.

She has the recognizable characteristics of the pin-up: abundant hair, youthful doll-like features and a bikini, but far from being suggestive she has more the hieratic air of a Byzantine virgin or the expressionless resignation of an Aunt Sally. She is also fully clothed by her 'tattoos' which for the most part are emblems of innocence: transfers of children, animals and flowers or cigarette cards with footballers. Transfers are a form of skin decoration or 'tattoo' favoured by children, hence the picture's title. Robert Melville has pointed out that Blake is not an advocate of the great majority, but a member of it. He is the one who collects the badges and puts Elvis again and again at the top of the hit parade. He has the faculty of growing up without shedding his childhood adolescence.   R.M.

Adolph Gottlieb 1903–1974
American School
BLAST 1960
Oil on paper, 78.5 × 56.5 cm
P.24–1966

The New York Times of 13 June 1943 carried a letter signed jointly by Adolph Gottlieb and Mark Rothko in which they put forward their reservations concerning the then prevalent Social Realist style and argue the merits of their own work:

'*We assert that the subject is crucial and only that subject-matter is valid that is tragic and timeless. That is why we profess spiritual kinship with primitive and archaic art.*'

During the 1940s and early 1950s Gottlieb's painting took the form of 'pictographs' whose themes were derived from classical myths. Symbols and images generated by the Surrealist technique of automatism – a kind of free associational drawing, Gottlieb organized within an informal grid. His notion of the validity of a theme or subject-matter depended upon that subject's ability to speak universally of man's condition. This he saw in 1943 as the spiritual degeneracy he believed had caused the Second World War. These concerns were precisely those of the psychologist Carl Gustav Jung. Jungian psychology is devoted to the understanding of the spiritual needs of Western civilization, and it was under Jung's influence that Gottlieb looked to primitive cultures for expressions of man's essential make-up before its suppression by 'Reason'. Like Jung, he identified myths as supranational expressions of archetypes – prototypic concepts shared by man regardless of culture or race.

By 1957 his interest in myth had shifted focus and in place of depicting mythic figures he began to examine the structures common to all myth. Contemporary theory accepted only one fundamental mythic structure, and this may have given impetus to his simplification of composition, beginning in this year the series generically known as *Bursts*, a theme that was to occupy him until his death.

In common with Rothko and other New York Colour Field painters, Gottlieb saw abstraction as a way of transcending everyday appearances and thus evading the finite associations with which he saw modern society enshrouding the environment.

Blast then is intended to signify the fundamental conflicts present in myth – conflicts that as Jung suggests are also present in the individual personality. In *Blast* the polarities are not specifically identified. A quiescent sphere hovers over a more mercurial component, in terms of the individual perhaps alluding to the dominance of reason; the geometric, and therefore conscious, above the unconscious. Concerning universal myth, in the opposition of red and black the allusion, if we accept the conventional colour symbolism of the group, is that of life contrasted with death; here austerely formulated according to principles first stated in the 1943 *Times* letter: 'We favour the simple expression of the complex thought.'

C.P.T.

Jean Dubuffet b.1901
French School
PAVOIS D'OREILLES
Signed and dated 1961
Wash, 42.7 × 33.3 cm
P.9–1964

Dubuffet came to painting relatively late in life at the age of about forty. In his artistic production Dubuffet sought contact with the common man. He rejected the artifice and sophistication of the work labelled 'Art' by the establishment.
An outsider himself without art school training, he developed a passionate interest in an unselfconscious art untainted by social concessions, cultural limits or taboos: the art of children, psychotics, mediums, amateurs. He sought to establish the validity of an 'individual creation without precedent', an art that was rough, raw, compulsive. These works he classified as *Art Brut*, and he adapted aspects of it to his own work, consciously exploiting its freedom and naturalism.

Pavois D'Oreilles ('Emblazoned With Ears') is a relatively late work but it demonstrates Dubuffet's continuing debt to *Art Brut*. The image is 'primitive' in the best sense, direct and vital: it is part of a tradition for seeking authenticity and inspiration in the primitive, the naive, the untutored, that goes back to Picasso and Gauguin. Physical realities are depicted without inhibition, and scale is distorted.

This frontally orientated vertical figure, its limbs placed symmetrically, is obviously related to the *Corps des Dames* of 1950–1, but the emphasis has changed. The deliberately imprecise contours of the figures in the earlier series have been replaced by a clearly defined silhouetted form, and the focus here is on head and limbs, not torso. Like a child Dubuffet emphasizes those features which have caught his eye or his imagination, and which for him, constitute the essence of his subject.

Dubuffet preferred amateur spontaneity to professional skill. He was fascinated by graffiti on walls ('the art of the ordinary man'). When he worked with oils he often incized the image into a thick layer of paint in direct imitation of graffiti. Even here, with only wash on paper, he has managed to create a good deal of textural interest. In the background the wash is uneven, puddled and thickened; on the figure a pale grey wash has been applied and then scrubbed and scratched to create a mottled effect in which the ground shows through.   G.M.S.

Tom Phillips b.1937
British School
MAP WALKS NOS.1 AND 2, 1972–3
Signed and dated lower right *Tom Phillips LXXII* and
Tom Phillips LXXIII
1: Acrylic on printed book page, 17.2 × 29 cm; 2: oil paint tint
on photograph, 17 × 29.1 cm
P.11–1977

Tom Phillips is one of the most creative and imaginative artists working in Britain today. His work encompasses many types of media, including painting, printmaking, music and writing, any or all of which may be used in a single work or project. His works always embody a central idea, or are the working-out of an idea, whose origin often lies in some everyday object or occurrence that the artist has noticed and whose context and implications he explores in the work. 'My passions are for structures, connections, correspondence, and systems which link the sensual, visual and intellectual worlds' (Tom Phillips. Works. Texts. To 1974. p.17). His work is in effect an invitation to explore with him the underlying structures and correspondences that he perceives in the world.

Map Walks Nos.1 and 2 is one of many projects in which he explores the structures and correspondences that he finds in the area of London in which he lives and works, Camberwell and Peckham. One project, *20 sites n years*, involves the annual photographing of twenty fixed sites on a half-mile radius from his home. This project is to be carried on by his children, and his children's children, into infinity – the 'n' years of the title. Another project, *The Walk to the Studio*, involves the study of the minutaie of material that lie in the short walk between his home and his studio. In these projects he draws our attention to minute changes in the town scenery, such as new traffic-signs or paving, or the sweet-wrappers lying in the street, things that might otherwise go unobserved, but for him have a history and significance of their own.

Map Walks Nos.1 and 2 are plans of a walking project in the area studied through two different sets of media. In this project 'a street walk is aerially designed to be elegant in itself. Sometimes sitting in an aeroplane one sees a street 'picked-out' because its lighting has (or has not) been modernized (ibid, p.126).' In the first map he has used the modern medium of acrylic paint on the actual pages of an A–Z of London to pick out those streets worthy of investigation. The background has deliberately been darkened and blurred to suggest the darkness of night, and the route indicated with brilliant cream paint to suggest the fluorescence of the sodium lamps in the street. On the second he has returned to the traditional medium of oil-paint but this time traces different, disconnected routes around the two areas of Peckham and Camberwell on a photograph of those same pages. He implies that there are innumerable possible walks contained in the map, and innumerable ways of recording them. He is inviting the spectator to try out these walks, and perhaps create some of his own. In this respect, the work of art is no longer the object that the museum possesses; what it owns is the framework for some active thought or participation by the spectator which is in itself the work of art.　　　　K.H.J.C.

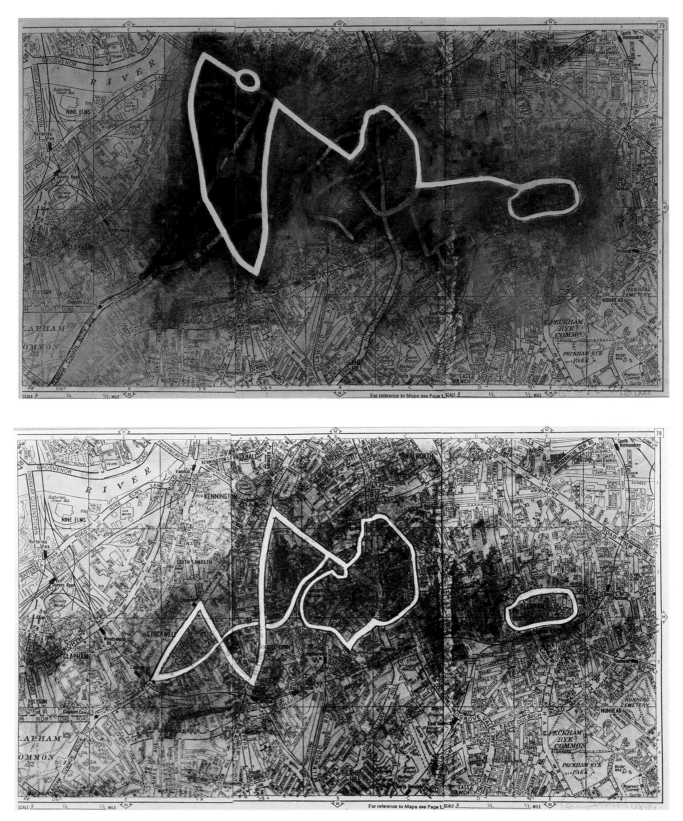

Richard Smith 1931
British School
FOUR KNOTS SERIES, NO.6 1975
Mixed media, 55.9 × 55.9 cm
P.24–1979

Four Knots Series, No.6 consists of one painted sheet of paper
folded along the direction of its vertical axis in two places,
and four pieces of string, threaded and tied so that the folded
edges are drawn together. Both vertical lines in the grid are
produced by the meeting edges, whereas the horizontal lines
are drawn in pencil. The lines that divide the format are thus
actual and apparent divisions – drawn edge, and edge itself –
and they are given equal functions in the dissection of the
surface. Through this juxtaposition Smith intends to disclose
the normally latent conventions and assumptions that
comprise the visual language of representation. Conventionally
line is used as a symbol for an edge. Here we have the reality
of edge contrasted with its representation in such a way that
the language is revealed as a system of symbols.

The avant garde of the 1960s and 1970s theorized that 20th-
century art had evolved, and should evolve, in the direction of
an explicit decoration of its essence. To the extent that his
work provides empirical evidence concerning the nature of
visual language, Smith's importance can be measured in
relation to this theoretical background. Yet in some ways his
painting operates very differently. Self-definition and efforts
towards maximum differentiation between the arts had
produced styles in painting and sculpture now called Minimal
Art. In this scheme painting was seen as having only two
dimensionality – flatness – as a unique property and all
references to objects and subjects outside of the painting itself
were proscribed.

Four Knots Series, No.6 evades and perhaps criticizes this
classification in its distortion of a flat plane into a three-
dimensional object with internal edges. Supplementing this is
the use of string and knots as constructive elements. Here the
allusion is to the packaging theme that has dominated Smith's
painting since the 1960s and which, in his own words,
has allowed him to remain 'close to the sensibility, ethos
almost, of objects and themes from present-day life.'   C.P.T.

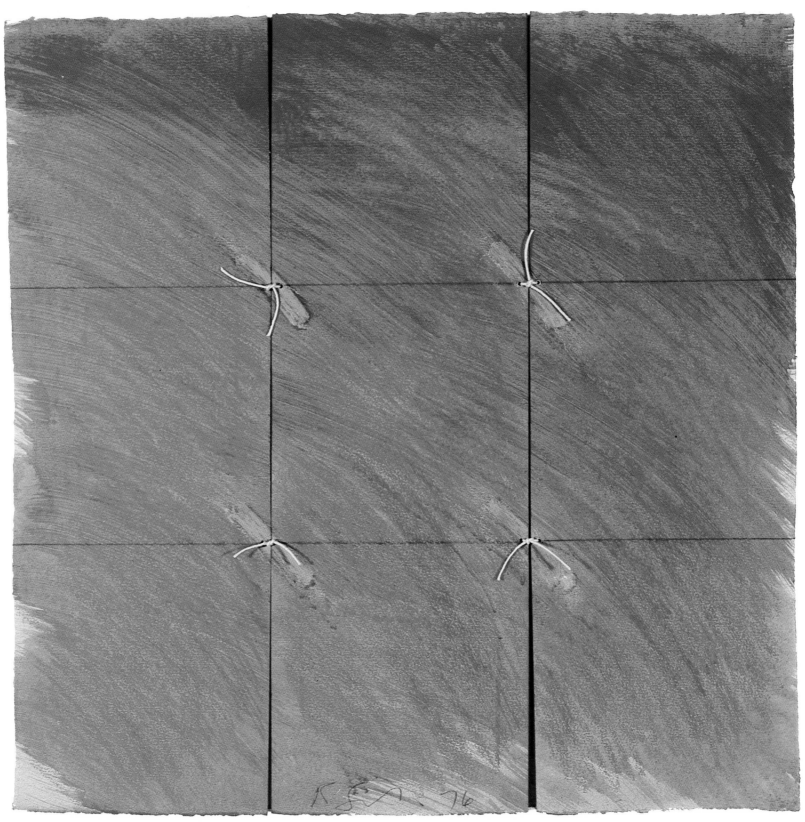

Index